WARREN TWP LIBRARY
42 MOUNTAIN BLVD

SEP 1 0 2008

WARREN, NJ 07059
908-754-5554

*T*his book is
dedicated
to all those
Little League coaches,
instructors, and parents
who put in so much
time to make sure a
new generation of
players enjoys the
game of baseball.

D1211690

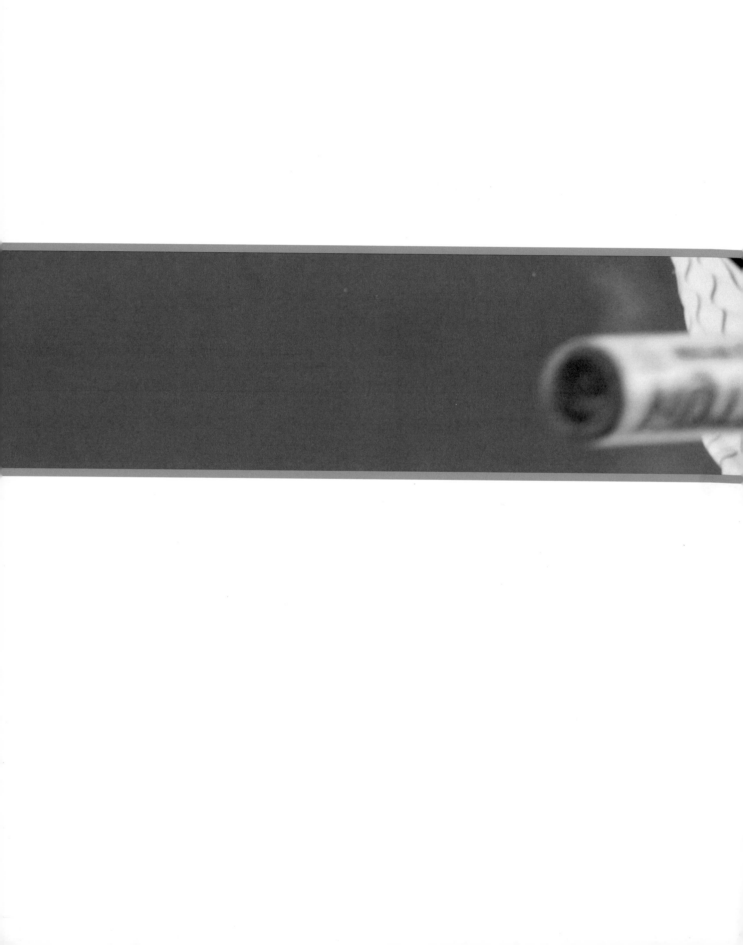

Coaching Youth Baseball

TEACHING HITTING FUNDAMENTALS

Developing Hitters with Character

SOMERSET CO. LIBRARY
BRIDGEWATER, N.J. 08807

BY KENNETH SIEGLER

Hitting consultation by David Trujillo

Photography by Jeff Carlick
Editing by Carol Whiteley
Design by David Hale
Printing by Hatcher Press

ISBN 978-0-9815362-0-0

This first edition published in March 2008 by
Ken Siegler, 924 Wilmington Way, Redwood City,
California 94062 USA.

Copyright© Kenneth Siegler, 2008

Printed in the United States

All rights reserved. With the exception of quoting brief passages for
the purpose of insuring the use of clear and precise baseball verbiage to describe an action or movement, no part of this publication may be reproduced without prior written permission from the
publisher.

The information in this book constitutes a best attempt to instruct
and teach baseball fundamentals and hitting. In no way does this
book guarantee any specific results nor define the one best way to
instruct or teach. The creators of this book do not guarantee that
similar verbiage or terminology could be used in other book publications to describe the game of baseball or how to instruct or teach.
All recommendations and instruction are made without any guarantee on the part of the author or any other party involved in the writing of this book, who also disclaims any liability incurred in
connection with the use of this data or specific materials.

Not all of the drills and exercises contained in this book are suitable
for everyone, and the use of this or any program could result in injury. Readers should consult a qualified professional to determine
which of these drills and/or exercises are suitable for a specific
individual.

Responsibility for any adverse effect or unforeseen consequences
resulting from information contained in this book is expressly
disclaimed.

The creators of this book recognize that some words, model names,
and designations, for example, mentioned herein are property of
the trademark holder. The creators of this book use them for identifi-
cation purposes only. This is not an official publication.

The book "Coaching Youth Baseball—Developing Hitters with
Character" is available in bulk for commercial or sales-promotional
use. For details write to Amazon.com.

ACKNOWLEDGMENTS

As any author will tell you, finding great people to work with is the most enjoyable part of writing a book. Thankfully, many wonderful people took time out of their busy schedules to help make this book a reality. Having such a wide array of professionals and children working with me inspired me to do the very best I could, and I appreciate their encouragement and their patience.

The following people and companies deserve recognition and thanks:

Beni Alfajora, Giulia Alfajora, Reynaldo Alfajora, Terry Clark, David Hale, John Robertson, Alicia Siegler, Jim Siegler, Carol Whiteley, Christopher Ede, Dylan Yapp, Kevin Yapp, Teri Yapp, Goetz Brothers Sporting Equipment, and to my good friend Steve Sprinkel at Hatcher Trade Press—great job on the printing.

Special thanks go to my immediate family: my beautiful wife Lenore and my wonderful daughter Jacqueline, who gave me the faith and support I needed to complete a project of this magnitude—I love you both more than words can say. I also send great thanks to my new friend Jeff Carlick, who I owe so much to for the incredible pictures he took—there would be no book without you, Jeff. Thank you also to David Trujillo, who's advice and consultation on hitting techniques and drills made sure the book had the best instruction.

Last but not least, I want to thank my wonderful eight-year-old son Troy, who put up with having his picture taken picture after picture, until the shot was just right. I'm very proud to call you my son, Troy, and hope some day that you will be lucky enough to share the joy of baseball with a family of your own.

BIOGRAPHIES

Ken Siegler

Ken Siegler has participated in San Francisco Bay Area sports since his childhood. He started coaching youth baseball in 2002 and became involved in numerous community and school sports programs, participating in a variety of roles. Today Ken coaches and manages Little League baseball teams in Redwood City, Calif., teaching a new generation of players, including his son Troy, about the joys of baseball.

Ken doesn't consider himself a baseball expert, but a devoted fan of the game who has spent many years helping children learn and develop the proper swing mechanics so that they too can enjoy the game. His goal with this book is to provide good leadership principles and to explain basic hitting techniques in a simple and straightforward way.

Ken is married to Lenore Siegler and has two children, Jacqueline, 11, and Troy, 8. Both children play several sports that keep mom and dad busy. Jacqueline especially enjoys club volleyball and Troy loves baseball, basketball, and tae kwan do.

Ken is a former senior executive with the Hewlett-Packard Company and currently is a business-solutions consultant for the technology industry. He holds a bachelor's degree from the University of California, Chico, with a concentration in business, and did graduate work at Babson College and Stanford University. His hobbies include travel, American Civil War history, and collecting and showing vintage American muscle cars.

David Trujillo

David Trujillo is a respected baseball instructor in the San Francisco Bay Area, where he makes his home. He is considered one of the best youth hitting specialists in the country and is also a personal fitness trainer for people of all ages, specializing in strength and conditioning for young athletes.

David holds a management degree in kinesiology from the University of Nevada, Las Vegas, where he

was named by the American Baseball Coaches Association First Team NCAA Division I Baseball All-American as a Designated Hitter. He was also an All-American in his senior year and was named to the ABCA First Team Region team. He hit .345 (79 for 242) with a team-high 18 home runs. In his junior year David was a second-team All-Conference first baseman while leading his team with a .374 batting average and setting a Mountain West Conference record with a 29-game hitting streak.

David was a star baseball and football player at Del Norte High School in New Mexico, where he lived with his parents Edward and Anita Trujillo and his four brothers and one sister. David considers his brother Tom to be the greatest influence on his career as an athlete.

Today, David has his own baseball instruction program and has coached some of the most talented youth baseball players in the country.

David would like to thank his beautiful fiancé, Olivia Camilleri, for all her love and support.

Troy Siegler

Troy Siegler is the son of Ken and Lorene Siegler and the young player photographed throughout this book doing drills. Troy is eight years old and a fifth-generation Californian who likes just about every sport. He is a red belt in tae kwan do and loves to play baseball, basketball, golf, and pool as well as to bowl and swim. Troy is a great son with a good sense of humor who cares for his family and friends. He respects others and knows that school comes first. And he loves his Nintendo DS.

Jeff Carlick

Jeff Carlick began his sports photography career at Cal State Fullerton, where he completed a BA degree in communications in 1982. He has worked at several newspapers in Southern California as a sports writer and sports photographer and freelanced for The Sporting News, Sport Magazine, and Street & Smith's Annual sports publications. He has photographed many major sports events, including two World Series, two NBA Finals, as well as Stanley Cup playoffs and National Football League Championship games. In 1992, Carlick moved to the Bay Area and worked as a contract photographer for Pinnacle Brands Trading Cards, shooting Major League Baseball and National Football League games. Carlick continues to freelance for Major League Baseball Properties and National Basketball Association Entertainment. He started his own business photographing youth sports in 2006.

Carol Whiteley

Carol Whiteley has been a writer and an editor in the San Francisco Bay Area for more than 20 years. She has written six nonfiction books on a variety of subjects, including creative writing; revised several manuscripts for publication; and written articles, on everything from gift giving to police work, that have been published in numerous magazines and newspapers, including Open Hand, The Washington Post, The San Francisco Examiner, The Baltimore Sun, and The San Jose/Silicon Valley Business Journal. Carol is a partner in Writing Doctor, an online writing and editing service (www.writingdoctor.com). She offers ghostwriting, copywriting, book proposal writing, editing, coaching, evaluation, proofreading, screenwriting, and other publishing services to individuals and corporate clients.

David Hale

David Hale is a designer and an art director with more than 35 years of experience in magazine and book publishing, advertising, and corporate design. He enjoys working with a variety of enterprises, including educational and trade publishers; technology businesses, from start-ups to multinationals; and local organizations ranging from organic farms to social service agencies.

TABLE OF CONTENTS

INTRODUCTION

Let Them Dream— And Help Them Grow

As a young boy growing up in the San Francisco Bay Area, I loved the game of baseball. I played almost every day during the spring and summer, and every night dreamed about the fun I would have doing it all over again the next day. My friends and I pretended to be our favorite professional baseball players, making amazing plays that would win the World Series in the bottom of the ninth. As a child, playing baseball was both my passion and my dream.

As I got older, I learned how to play the game right, with the help of several great coaches and mentors. Now I coach youth baseball myself, with the goal of helping the next generation not only learn game fundamentals but enjoy the game and dream their own dreams while feeling like a superstar.

Living dreams and having fun are what baseball is all about. I tell parents at the first team meeting that there are no seven- or eight-year-olds in the Baseball Hall of Fame, and that most children who play organized baseball will not play at the high school or college interscholastic level, let alone become major league superstars. That means we need to concentrate on making sure each child has a Hall of Fame experience now, and that, whatever career path children pursue, they will all benefit from being happy, confident, compassionate, and hardworking, which playing youth baseball will help them become.

As you take on the responsibilities of being a coach or mentor, then, it's important that you not only encourage children to dream big, but help them have fulfilling, enriching baseball experiences today that will enable them to learn and grow. Rather than be-

Coaching Goals

• *To properly teach baseball fundamentals*—Knowing the basic skills will help players succeed.

• *To develop character in young players*—Having integrity will enable them to respect themselves and others.

• *To enjoy the game and have your team have fun*—Having fun motivates learning and makes the experience positive.

• *To have players recognize the value of preparation and dedication*—It's good to have far-reaching goals but also to take care of details.

• *To engage players' hearts and souls*—If you believe, they will follow.

• *To help players achieve and be the best they can be*—Goals need to have personal value.

• *To motivate players to be future leaders*—What you teach today will help children tomorrow.

come a coach or mentor to develop youngsters into major leaguers, or to have the best team in your league, I hope you will become a coach or mentor with goals like those above.

Youth baseball is a developmental league in which learning and fun are key, and your coaching philosophy should echo that—the way you coach and lead will influence your players' enjoyment, understanding, and respect for the game and for other players. Of course, a coach also needs to know how to appropriately teach baseball fundamentals, which is a primary criterion of success. However, it is equally important for coaches to recognize honest efforts regardless of their results and to be able to help players deal with failure. Doing so will help children grow into confident and caring adults who will then help future generations meet with the same success.

A good coach or baseball mentor, then, needs to have passion for the game and the desire to develop character in children. Good coaches teach compassion, dedication, respect, responsibility, comradeship, and good sportsmanship. Although baseball is a game at its

core, when coached correctly it is also a tool for developing character. Coaching, therefore, should be about maximizing each player's potential and experience.

Imagine for a moment you are coaching a Little League game. One of your players hits a ball over the third baseman's head and it rolls into the outfield and keeps on rolling until the player reaches home plate. To that young hitter, the joy he or she experiences is very much like the joy a 35-year-old superstar feels when he hits a home run in the bottom of the ninth to win the game. Baseball is about the moment, but it's also about experiences that both children and adults can savor and that can last throughout their lives. I hope you experienced a baseball moment that is still with you today. If you did, think back to the coach or teacher who helped make that experience possible and who helped guide you to become the person you are now. Think about following in that person's footsteps.

Good coaching helps prepare children for adulthood. It gives young players a great opportunity to not only realize their dreams but gain the ability to deal positively with unmet expectations. Regardless of how your team ranks at the end of the season, you will be there to make sure your players are humble in victory and gracious in defeat. You'll also be there to remind them that failure is only a detour to success and that people don't fail in life unless they stop trying.

To help you achieve your goals, this book is divided into four parts: "Being a Good Coach," which talks about how to lead successfully, provide a positive experience, and put together and run a successful program; "Teaching Hitting Fundamentals," which shows you and your staff and parents how to help players properly grip the bat, develop the correct stance, develop an efficient, repeatable swing, and make base hits; "Leading Practice Drills," which provides a variety of proven practice drills; and

"Resources," which offers additional information to help you successfully lead your team.

As a coach of four- to ten-year-olds, you have the opportunity to make a big difference in their lives. I urge you not to waste it. I also urge you to put this book's principles and ideas to work and to go out there and have fun!

PART 1

Being a Good Coach

To be a good Little League coach, you need to combine the inspirational with the nitty-gritty. You need to be a strong leader, provide a positive experience, and handle the varied tasks that go into managing a team.

CHAPTER 1

Leading Successfully

Before any manager, coach, or parent begins to teach baseball fundamentals, he or she should have a good understanding of what it takes to be a good leader of this age group. I believe it takes the same critical elements that are needed to be good at any leadership position: being fair and consistent, communicating effectively, taking appropriate responsibility, using good organizational skills, keeping participants safe, setting reasonable expectations and goals, encouraging and building strong relationships, leading by example, and developing a successful teaching strategy.

Being Fair and Consistent

Although the ideas in this book will go a long way in helping you handle the many variables that are part of youth baseball, there will be many times when you encounter a situation for which there are no league-sanctioned rules or guidelines. Therefore it's important that, before your first practice, you decide on—and write down—your own set of rules and guidelines. Be sure that these rules are consistent with any set by the league. Remember, the manager runs the team (see page 23 for more on the role of manager), so any rules need to support his or her directives. This is not negotiable, and will affect the team's ability to develop a good reputation.

Once the team has an established set of rules and guidelines (see "Encouraging and Building Relatin-ships" in this chapter to help you build and establish your own), have assistant coaches, parent volunteers, and any other adults involved approve the rules for the season. At the first practice, read the rules to the players and make sure they understand them.

Once practices get underway, you'll be very glad you took the time to lay your rules down. Still, you're almost certain to come up against situations that you didn't count on. For example, at the beginning of one season, I did not have a rule about eating on the bench during games. It never occurred to me that such a thing could become a major distraction! But during the first game, the bench housed a smorgas-bord of snacks: candy, sunflower seeds, sandwiches, you name it. The bench was a mess and the kids' energy levels rocketed from up to down, depending on their sugar intake. Even when the bench coach confis-cated the food, more appeared without the players even moving. I finally asked some of the kids where the team's bounty of nutrition was coming from. They said their mothers were concerned that they hadn't eaten before play started and didn't want them to be hungry. Since our games began at 5:00 p.m. and ended around 6:30, this was a legitimate concern.

After speaking with the parents I decided that the players could have a light snack before the game and water during the game. We also designated one family per game to bring pizza after the game. This not only prevented parents from worrying about children's hunger pangs and having to rush home after the game to feed starving players, but it built team unity and gave the coaches a chance to speak with parents and players about how the team played. It also kept the bench uncluttered and helped to keep the kids on a more even keel.

Whenever a situation arises for which you have no set rules, the best thing to do is simply listen to the people involved and learn what is happening—listen first and act second. When you act, be sure that you act fairly, not with bias, and note down whatever it is that you do so that you can do the same thing if the same or a similar situation comes up again. If the situation warrants, also send an e-mail about it to the entire team, letting everyone know what step or steps you took to resolve the problem. Also be ready to discuss the issue openly and to accept constructive input to make the situation better.

Communicating Effectively

Communication is not just about talking to players and their parents, teaching the fundamentals, and having a good game plan. It's all of that, but it is also about meeting with league officials, managers, and other coaches before the season starts and keeping lines of communication open all season long to avoid misunderstandings and problems.

Before the season begins, hold a meeting with your coaching staff. In this meeting, have all participants discuss what they hope to accomplish during the season. These goals should be in line with the league and with parent expectations that each player should play every position during the season and be a team captain for at least one game.

It's also important to communicate with parents early on—you'll be amazed at how educating them ahead of time helps in the resolution of the majority of

issues that develop regarding fair play and participation. A good way to keep coach-parent communication strong is to designate a team mom or dad to get out weekly e-mails to all parents showing the rotation of players, innings played, and other important facts.

It's also important to set up a chain of resolution in which parents address issues with you first and then, if necessary, with the commissioner of your division and, last, league officials. Encourage parents to come to you with problems by telling them that if you don't know the problem exists you won't be able to address it; one of the most frustrating things for Little League coaches as well as board members is having parents say at the end of the season that they wish something had been done differently. Ask parents to make any complaints specific and objective. The idea is to have everyone have a good experience, and often discussing an issue in person leads to that outcome.

Taking Appropriate Responsibility

A good coach doesn't assume that parents and assistant coaches understand all that is required of them to make the season run smoothly. With people so busy these days, you will need to make sure that all the many tasks of managing a team are carried out. This doesn't mean that you or a select few need to do everything and run the risk of burning out and not enjoying being part of the team. Yes, you're in charge, but recruiting as many parent volunteers as needed will help everyone involved share the work as well as the fun, and give you the time you need to concentrate on coaching. Ask parents to help early and ask them often.

Most parents won't feel overburdened taking on one or two small tasks that don't involve developing drills or game-related preparation activities, such as bringing snacks or making a team banner. Recruit a team mom or dad as soon as possible to coordinate and assign responsibilities. Work with that person to develop a chart to plot season-long requirements of what needs to be done when. Encourage the coordinator to use e-mail to facilitate signups and continuing communication.

Many parents will also enjoy helping you run practices. Instead of watching practices, they may relish the opportunity to get involved and be part of the fun and action. Ask parents if any of them are interested in helping with batting practice, leading warm-up exercises, shagging fly balls, or making sure that players get down on ground balls. Doing so will not only bring them enjoyment, but allow you and the assistant coaches to work with the kids on the finer points of baseball fundamentals.

Using Good Organizational Skills

When your organizational skills are poor, everyone you work with suffers, especially you. Coaches who come to practice without a plan are setting up themselves—and their team—for disaster. Without a plan, you can spend as much as 70% of a practice running around thinking about what to do next. If this happens to you, your players will notice very quickly and convert the field into a playground while you try to come up with a neat drill. Although some coaches minimize the importance of being organized, and believe that all that matters is that the kids have fun, nothing could be further from the truth. Children (and their parents) invest a large chunk of time in learning how to play baseball, and you will be cheating them if you're not prepared to coach.

Not being prepared will also result in your spending many a night taking phone calls from parents about the right way to run practices, which is the last thing you want to have happen. Instead, spend some time well before each practice developing a plan (see page xx for a sample practice plan), then e-mail it to all coaches, players, and parents. This will show everyone that you and your assistants care about creating the best possible experience for the players. Providing a well-organized practice will also eliminate player boredom and downtime and, if you stick to your plans, your players should learn quickly. Teams that practice well also usually win their games.

Keeping Players Safe

For most leagues, it is mandatory that players receive physical clearance before participating in baseball activities. Before the season starts, have your players checked out by their doctor and ask parents to tell you about any areas of potential concern, for example, if their child has asthma or a severe allergy. I also recommend that you have parents or legal guardians sign a participation agreement and also a consent form that allows their child to be treated by a qualified care

provider in case of an emergency. (See Appendix C for a sample consent form.)

In addition to being physically fit enough to play baseball, young players need to play in a safe environment—a baseball field in disrepair is just an accident waiting to happen. If the one you'll practice and play on is in poor condition it will need to be groomed and cleaned before you let the team use it. This can be a lot of work, but it's critical to having fun and playing safely.

Before each practice and game, arrive 15 to 20 minutes early and inspect the field and your equipment. Have players and parent volunteers help you rake the infield, free it of debris, and mark areas of the outfield that have large divots or potholes. Report any hazards that you are unable to fix rather than leave them for the next team to deal with. Also make sure that the batter's box, the on-deck circle, and the first- and third-base coaching areas are clear and properly marked and that all the bases are properly installed.

Last but not least, take the time to check uniforms and practice attire. Any loose material that inhibits a player's movement should be taken care of before play and all players should wear rubber baseball cleats when on the field. Be sure that boys wear a cup

A player should always wear a helmet when he is at bat in practice or in a game.

to protect the groin area and that all helmets, bats, balls, and the catcher's gear are in good condition.

Appendix B lists the basic equipment you will need to successfully work with young baseball players. Many leagues have equipment boxes on site that house the major items, but if your field doesn't have one or important pieces are missing, notify your league director.

It is important to make sure the field is maintained properly to provide a safe environment for the players.

Setting Reasonable Expectations and Goals

One of the big differences between leading and managing is that leaders need to have the ability to listen, compromise, and adapt in order to do things better. Children between the ages of four and ten vary greatly in their physical and emotional development and many just won't be ready for particular exercises and drills. To be a good leader you will need to modify your coaching methods and your expectations and goals to suit your team. This means evaluating each child's ability before putting together a practice plan.

A good way to start your evaluation, before the first practice, is to check every child's sign-up sheet for age, experience, and any learning challenges. Also check in with parents early on to find out their expectations. As you evaluate players, be sure not to compare one to another regarding mastery of objectives. Each child should be evaluated based on his or her own developmental level and improvement.

Once you have an understanding of your team's makeup, think about and talk with your assistant coaches about what appropriate expectations should be. For example, expectations might include: Know the rules of the game, be a team player, practice a winning attitude, and find out what each player does best and what each needs to work on. Then organize a team meeting, including parents, to cover expectations as well as the agenda items listed above and any others you deem necessary. It's a good idea to provide the written information in binders that families can take home.

Team goals are always more important than individual goals. If you disagree, then coaching baseball may not be right for you. As I've said, teammates are co-dependent—if only a few succeed, then the team does not succeed, and games become opportunities to showcase the skills of only a few.

However, individual goals are also important. All young players want to do well and have a good time, and everyone involved with their team wants them to do that too. No player wants to fail, so it is up to coaches and parents to appropriately define success in baseball.

Team Kick-off Meeting Agenda
1. Manager, coaches, and team coordinator (a parent volunteer) introductions
2. Player and family introductions
3. League rules
4. Practice schedule and game schedule
5. League events
6. Health forms and confirmation of age
7. List of contact information
8. Coaches' expectations

For children aged four through ten, the most important goal is to enjoy playing the game; if they don't have fun, it's very unlikely they will play more than two or three years before moving on to something else. But in addition to having fun, they should also learn some key skills, all of which can be mastered with proper coaching and practice. Your local Little League officials should be able to direct you to additional reference material for points not covered in this book.

Goals for Four- to Six-Year-Olds
1. Learn the basic elements of the game: the right direction to run when the ball is hit, that run-

ners must touch the bases, the way outs are made (catching the ball in the air when it's hit, throwing to first, or tagging the runner), to run past first base when you're the batter, scoring a run, and that three outs constitute an inning.

2. Learn throwing mechanics: turning your body so that the front shoulder points toward the target, keeping the elbow above the shoulder, and stepping toward the target with the non-throwing foot while releasing the ball.

3. Learn tracking: following the ball into the glove with your eyes, whether it's on the ground or in the air; using two hands to catch and field; and catching the ball out in front of your body.

4. Learn hitting: how to hold and swing the bat, batting safety (knowing when not to swing a bat and to wear a batting helmet), hitting off a tee, and hitting softly tossed pitches. (See Part 2 for extensive information about hitting.)

5. Learn to play the position: to let your buddy field a ball that is hit to him or her and to be aggressive and go after the ball when it is hit to you.

6. Learn to respect teammates and coaches.

Goals for Seven- to Ten-Year-Olds

1. Learn all of the above.

2. Learn more advanced elements: how to make force-outs, how to tag up, base running (when you don't have to run, not running past your teammates on the base paths), and distinguishing balls and strikes.

3. Learn more advanced throwing mechanics: the four-seam grip; pointing the front shoulder, stepping, and throwing; and generating momentum toward the target and following the throw.

4. Learn catching and fielding techniques: handling thrown and hit balls, catching with fingers up versus fingers down, seeing the glove and the ball, using two hands, forehands and backhands, the underhand flip, first-base fundamentals, and crossovers and drop steps.

5. Learn more advanced hitting techniques: choosing the right bat, the proper grip, hitting pitched balls, and drill work for batting practice. (Part 2 of this book concentrates on the batting stance; Part 3 provides hitting drills.)

6. Learn positional play: the position and areas each player should cover, how to cover the nearest base when the ball is not hit to you, and the basics of cutoffs and relays.

Goals for Players Preparing for the Next Level

1. Learn the basic rules, including the infield fly rule and the rule about balks.

2. Learn about base running: leads, steals, and extra base hits.

3. Learn more advanced pitching and throwing mechanics: the windup versus the stretch; the four-seam grip; how to shuffle, throw, and follow; the pitcher covering first.

4. Learn more advanced hitting techniques: repetitive hitting and handling advanced hitting drills and bunting.

5. Learn more advanced elements: cutoffs and relays], basic bunt defenses, basic first-and-third situations, underhand flips and double plays, defending the steal, and infield and outfield communication and priorities.

For additional help teaching these skills, check the Little League Official Regulations and Playing Rules at www.LittleLeague.org.

Encouraging and Building Relationships

To have a successful and fun season it is important to remember that you, your staff, and your players make up a team and that teams succeed only when they work together. All participants should be encouraged to respect, listen to, and support each other at all times. One of the best ways to encourage that goal is to make sure that each team member knows his or her role. Sometimes, of course, one person may play multiple roles.

Role of the Manager

1. Is the ultimate authority on all matters related to the team

2. Sets batting order, fielding positions, and pitching rotation

3. Assigns base and bench coaches

4. Is the spokesperson to the league on all team matters

5. Ensures that league rules and regulations are known and enforced

Leading

6. Is responsible for the safety of players and coaches

7. Sets practice schedules and coordinates game schedules

8. Is responsible for keeping parents and league officials informed and resolving parent and coaching concerns in a timely, polite manner

9. Instructs and mentors coaching staff

10. Teaches and mentors players

11. Creates a fun and positive environment

Role of the Coach

1. Assists manager with day-to-day responsibilities

2. Helps organize and prepare field

3. Coaches bases and or bench

4. Runs drills and coordinates practices

5. Teaches and mentors players

6. Ensures the safety of players

7. Monitors pitch counts or pitches to players

8. Is accessible to parents and answers parent questions in a timely and polite manner

9. Creates a fun and positive environment

Role of the Player

1. Respects and listens to coaches, other players, and other teams

2. Follows safety rules

3. Arrives on time ready to play

4. Practices well in order to play well

5. Exhibits good sportsmanship

6. Cleans up and puts away equipment

7. Hustles at all times

8. Supports teammates

9. Practices for one hour each week outside of team practices

10. Has a positive attitude and wants to have fun

Role of the Parent

1. Works with child at least once a week

2. Gets involved as a volunteer

3. Shows up for games and practices

4. Understands and respects the rules of the game

5. Informs manager or coach of issues that need addressing in a timely manner

6. Doesn't pressure the child—let the child have fun

7. Helps child win and lose graciously

8. Has fun and stays relaxed

9. Provides proper health coverage (dental and medical) for the child

10. Makes sure the child comes to practices and games

11. Respects the manager and coaches

Everyone involved with the team is also part of a larger family, which includes other coaches, managers, and teams as well as league officials. As a leading part of that family, it's important that you take the time to get to know your league officials and other coaches in your division. Doing so will not only bring you more support but it will make game planning easier and conflict resolution faster and less antagonistic. It's also important to keep your sense of humor and to have a realistic perspective. When issues arise, remember to take the high road and to never show up a player, coach, or parent in front of others. One of your goals should be to develop positive relationships with everyone and to make your league one of the best and most enjoyable to play in.

Leading by Example

Good sportsmanship and a sense of dignity are easy to exhibit when your team is functioning well and winning. However, they can both be more difficult to come by when your team is not executing and is losing. In times of disappointment, when expectations fall short, parents, other coaches, and especially your players will look to you to see how to handle adversity. Will you be angry, sad, and quiet at those times, or calm, upbeat, and confident?

No matter the circumstances, a good coach remains upbeat and positive, always remembering that baseball is a game and that everyone involved will take home the physical and verbal messages the coach relays. A good coach also remembers that winning is not the goal, but that playing your best is.

Make sure you stay patient and understanding during a tough game. Young players can be sensitive to perceived pressure to perform and may put additional pressure on themselves, making the game a chore rather than fun. Mental and physical mistakes are staples of developmental league baseball, so it's important not to get on kids' cases and to keep in mind that losses are just detours on the way to success. When players make mistakes, they watch to see how others react. If you and your coaching staff and the other players say there's no problem, players will be encouraged to get back into action and try again.

Always finish a tough game or practice with a laugh, a smile, and an anecdote or two about how things will be better the next time out. And always lead by example, showing your team, your coaching staff, and parents what class and dignity are all about.

Developing a Successful Teaching Strategy

Baseball is a game of subtle movements and positioning, so it's key that players understand the importance of proper form and balance. If we teach young players the wrong techniques, it will take a long time to correct them. And although many young players can get by with poor form at the Little League level, it may keep them from competing well later on. It's critical that coaches communicate the right skills early on to make playing the game much easier and to give the kids a greater chance of success.

An effective way to become a good coach and teacher is to enroll in a couple of baseball workshops that provide first-timer information and/or refresher classes on the correct way to coach and run drills. You may also want to line up a respected baseball professional or college player, perhaps retired, who can teach the finer aspects of the game to you, your assistants, and your players right at the start.

When you teach skills, repeat the exercises again and again until they become second nature to the players (for an extensive list of hitting drills, see Part 3). However, also make sure to break drills up and to make them fun so players don't get bored. Repetition is important, but so is moderation in building an athlete who is successful over the long term. We do not want to coach like the old Soviet Union coaches did, with the goal of finding an athlete at a very young age who they could develop into a world-dominating champion. By teaching the basic concepts to young children in a relaxed and enjoyable way, we will have a larger and better population of quality ball players.

When leading an exercise, explain the elements of the drill in small groups or stations and relate how each element will benefit each player. If you're organized and communicate well, your team will move quickly along. You can also let players lead certain elements of practice under your direction—it will not only be fun for everyone but build players' confidence and leadership.

Once the team has mastered a drill, you can feel comfortable asking parents to assist you in running it. Rotate parent participation whenever possible and communicate with parents effectively to cut down on questioning you during practice. End practices by having the team run the bases for time and accuracy. Young players love to show off how fast they are, and running will help them go home tired and happy.

CHAPTER 2

Having a Successful Experience

In youth baseball, team success, rather than individual success, is key. But what does team success mean? A team succeeds when players develop character and believe not only in themselves but in the other players on the team. Statistics and personal recognition take a back seat to the satisfaction that is felt from being part of a team and from working together to reach a goal. Winning is more enjoyable and losing is easier to deal with as part of a team rather than as an individual.

To help your team succeed, encourage your young players to help each other, especially to support players who are having a hard time. Young players who show compassion will forget about their own failures and gain strength and respect from helping others. Being compassionate and learning to work together will not only build individual character but improve team chemistry and interpersonal relationships. Working as a team will also minimize negative thinking and prevent individual players from taking on undue burdens related to a team loss. It will also keep young players who don't deal well with failure from wanting to quit.

Individual success is always exciting and special but it should be recognized as an action that helps the team improve. For example, say a hitter gets on base by being walked. The next batter hits a ball to the right side of the infield for an out but advances the base runner to second. The third batter flies out to center but the runner on second tags up and takes third on the third base coach's instruction. The manager then notices that the third baseman is playing well off the bag and gives this information to the first base coach, who relays it to the next batter. At the same time the third base coach reminds the runner on third that there are two outs and he should run on contact. The batter then proceeds to hit one down the third base line. The third baseman stops the ball but can't make the play since he's playing too far off the bag. The runner scores and the player who was up gets the run batted in. The box score shows an RBI for one player, but it took three other players and three coaches—plus practice, thinking ahead, and strategy—for the play to succeed. It took teamwork.

In the example, every ball that was hit to score a run was caught by the opposing team, yet the run still scored. As a manager or coach, it can be hard to teach young players the importance of supporting their teammates or playing within a team concept when parents cheer only for the end result or when their child is up to bat. Part of team success involves reminding parents that developmental baseball is all about teamwork and that for their child to be successful everyone else needs to contribute. In baseball terms this is called setting the table.

Celebrating the Effort

Too often in youth sports, the final score is what's emphasized. This can be frustrating to children who don't master drills quickly and whose game efforts don't show up as a base hit or a ground ball. Recognizing true effort and defining good results are therefore essential to having every player achieve and celebrate success on the baseball diamond.

Early in the season, define a set of parameters that you and the coaching staff will use to recognize positive effort and show that goals are being reached.

When managing or coaching, always focus on the effort and on positive ways to reinforce the idea of success. In addition, always celebrate each small success and congratulate each player after every game, win or lose.

Here's an example of a time when focusing on effort helped a young player feel better about himself and improve his skills. During one particular season, a player on my team was incredibly good at catching ground balls. Whenever the ball was hit his way, he would always stay low to the ground with hands touching the ground in front, like a bulldozer ready to scoop. The problem was that after he caught the ball, he would throw it like a rocket—anywhere but toward the target. It didn't take long for his teammates to shy away from his throws, and he quickly became nervous and upset when he played. He either didn't want to play the infield or, if he did play there, he would hold onto the ball until there was a forced out near the position he was playing.

I decided to hold a practice in which the kids would lob as many baseballs as they could into a bucket 30 feet away. The rules were that if you got the ball into the bucket with an overhand throw, you received two points. If you hit the bucket with the ball, you got one point. And if you threw the ball 10 feet in front of or beyond the bucket, you would lose a point. If the players as a team got 50 points, they would not need to do any throwing drills that day.

During the practice, not only did the kids have a lot of fun, but, more importantly, the child who had been having a hard time throwing made a great effort to throw more accurately and with less power. As he learned to control the ball, his teammates saw that he could throw the ball well and with less force, and he began to feel better about himself. By focusing on learning, the young player overcame his throwing challenges and both he and his teammates gained the confidence to stick with it and help each other.

In addition to effort, good results can be achieved when young players bring their personal touch and style to the game. Encourage your team to look the part of professional baseball players with colored gloves, armbands, particular cleats, and a certain way of wearing their pants. The kids should have clean uniforms, tuck in their shirts, and use equipment that is safe, but dressing like a real baseball player will give them confidence as they play. Players will also gain confidence if you find something special in each of them to celebrate.

Playing "No Blame" Games

Part of having a successful experience is taking responsibility for your actions. It is never too early to teach young players that they are accountable for what they do and the way they act. In baseball, there are many opportunities for young players to find reasons for not succeeding: "The ball was thrown too low." "The sun was in my eyes." "The ground is uneven." "I lost my hat." "My favorite bat was missing." "Billy keeps poking me when I'm on the bench." Teach your players that despite distractions they can play the game and be successful. When they're having a hard time, point out some things they did well as well as obstacles they overcame to help them avoid playing the blame game.

One word of caution here: Make sure you listen carefully to your young players' concerns to be certain that what's keeping them from succeeding is not a serious physical problem or a confidence issue. Get to know your players so you understand who they are and what motivates them.

Answering Players' Questions

Children will ask you many questions during the season, ranging from the funny to the very insightful. It's important to answer all of them because questions of any sort show that players are interested and they enable kids to learn. Your answers will also help to establish your credibility and encourage the coach-player connection.

When you answer questions, make your explanations as simple and specific as you can, using wording appropriate to the age level. Children take direction literally, and need to understand exactly what to do. That understanding, of course, will help players develop more rapidly and become excited about pushing their limits. To help young players have a good experience, don't worry about how well they execute a drill but concentrate instead on how well they understand what they need to do.

Recognizing Players' Success

The carrot or the stick? That is the question many coaches ask themselves when considering how to motivate young players. A coach's behavior and belief system set the tone for his or her team, and my philosophy is to be honest, consistent, and to lead by example. It is also to encourage, support, and recognize effort rather than to put pressure on or evoke fear.

I also believe that the key to real success is having the ability to make others around you successful. If you think about the people who mentored you, you'll find that they made you feel wanted and valued by enabling you to be part of something special or to accomplish a goal. The same holds true for managing and coaching. Your success depends on having your team have a positive experience and the kids' success will come from every player contributing and working with others.

It is the responsibility of the manager and coaches to recognize all players' efforts and to explain to the team how each player's contribution enables everyone to succeed. So point out hard work during practices

Sleeve Badges
1. Batting Achievement Award = 10 hits or more during a season or reaching a personal goal set by the coach
2. Fielding Achievement Award = Fielding Certification, Basic Competency Level for the age group, in fielding, throwing, and catching, or reaching a personal goal set by the coach

Helmet Stickers
1. Runs batted in
2. Runs scored
3. Extra base hit
4. Stolen base or hustle
5. Great catch
6. Great effort
7. Great team spirit

and highlight special efforts as best practices after games. Also provide incentives to encourage players to strive to meet attainable goals. For example, I give out helmet stickers and sleeve badges (see page 29 for how I award them) when children accomplish a certain task or exhibit good sportsmanship, with the goal of finding something to reward every player for. I also distribute a monthly newsletter during the season that recognizes all players who contributed to the team.

Recognizing others and giving credit where credit is due will lead to a successful season for both you and your team. It will also enable you and your coaching staff to track the progress of players and to make recommendations, based on players' physical and emotional maturity, on ways they can improve in particular areas.

Managing Bad Attitudes, Hurt Feelings, and Negative Situations

As a coach, you will need to turn many challenging or negative situations into positives. At no time should you accept bad behavior or poor effort or let players think that it's alright to not be part of the team. When you see that something is wrong or not working, you will need to make decisions that put the team's best interests first.

For example, one year I had two players who felt it was their right to be heard any time they had something to say, even though a coach or another player was already speaking. Many times they wanted to speak to gain attention and or to be funny. After a few instances of this, I asked the players why they came to practice. One said his dad wanted him to be part of the team and both said that they had to be there. The next question I asked was, "Do you want to play baseball?" Both said yes, but that they didn't like practice and didn't think it was necessary—they both claimed they were very good players already! This resulted in lots of laughs from the other players.

I then asked both players to lead us in warm-ups, and asked parents attending practice to participate in the team stretching and running. I told the team that there were two rules: no one was to speak while the two players gave out directions, and we could not start until the two players enforced the first rule. Quickly the two players got frustrated trying to organize all the players, coaches, and parents. When I asked if they would like my assistance, they both said yes. So I agreed on one condition: that they would respect the team rules and would give 100% in practice. Both boys agreed.

I then organized everyone on the field and let the two players lead the warm-ups. After the exercises were completed, I asked what the two boys had learned and if they had enjoyed leading the team. Both players said they had liked the practice because they both had felt important and had learned that it was important to respect and work with the coaches and the other players. The lesson was not wasted on the parents either. When the coaching staff asked the parents to speak to their children about the importance of respect and how fun practices could be if everyone participated, they jumped right in, having seen it for themselves. At the end of the practice, the coaching staff gave the two players 100%-effort stickers to put on their helmets, which motivated the other players to listen, abide by the rules, and become team leaders.

In addition to helping players learn to respect and work with others, a coach at this level also needs to be sensitive to how young players feel and how they respond to playing the game. When a player's feelings get hurt, you need to speak to him or her one on one at eye level to find out what happened and to figure out to solve the problem. It is very easy to read a child's face and body language if you take the time to observe.

If player conflict is the cause of hurt feelings, make sure the players involved speak to each other and apologize with a handshake. If the cause is that a coach or parent tried to correct the player's physical or mental mistake, the player may not only have hurt feelings but feel he or she is letting that authority figure down. Whatever the cause, be sure to listen carefully to what's on the player's mind and to explain why correction is important. Recognize and identify issues early and show compassion and respect resolving them.

Keeping Players Motivated

What young child doesn't like to pick up a stick and hit something with it? Add in some throwing, running, and catching and you're very likely to have kids having a great time. Enjoyment can lessen, though, when adults try to organize and monitor these actions. Part of having a successful experience is convincing your young players that doing baseball-related actions well will make it even more fun to go out to the ball field—and doing well takes practice, practice, practice.

As you implement your coaching philosophy and practices, do your players move quickly on the field? Are they interested in what you are saying? Is there a lot of team interaction? Does the practice fly by? Do you stay after practice because the kids won't take no for an answer?

Practice Tips

1. Practice in small groups.
2. Hold action-oriented drills (see the drills in Part 3).
3. Provide a variety of activities (hitting, running, throwing, and catching).
4. Recognize and reward effort.
5. Have every player participate equally.
6. Remember that coaching is 80% physical (demonstrating) and 20% mental (providing information by speaking to the players).
7. Be specific in your directions.
8. Ask players to show what they learned.
9. Make notes on what is working.

If the answer to all of these questions is yes, keep up the good work. But if your players appear bored or unhappy, it's time to make adjustments. Children have limited attention spans and a "routine rut" can put them to sleep. Follow the practice tips to keep your players motivated to learn and focus on the big picture.

In addition, always have a good time and enjoy the amazing things you see on the field. There are many entertaining moments to be had when coaching youth baseball!

Keeping Players Strong

In most cases, children are in satisfactory shape to play or practice the game of baseball. However, muscular and cardio fitness are critical for the hitting, running, and spurts of speed baseball requires, and maintaining strength, endurance, and flexibility should be a staple of any practice program. Players who have greater muscular fitness will have a better chance of reaching their potential, be less likely to sustain an injury, and recover more quickly if they are hurt.

To keep kids strong, have them start practices by warming up for 15 minutes with light running, stretching, and calisthenics (see page 36 for a sample practice plan); while children are generally limber, they can become tight just like adults. Have them finish practice sessions by running the bases and then sitting down to catch their breath while you review what you covered and make any announcements. Throughout the practice take water breaks (and keep water at drill stations) to ensure that players stay hydrated, and watch out for players who seem short of breath or show signs of fatigue. Children will push themselves, so keep a good watch, especially on hot days and if your field has little or no shade.

Helping Players Improve

Coaches usually do not get trophies or awards. What we get is much more important: seeing players improve, often significantly, and build confidence. But because all players have different strengths and weaknesses, to help them improve it is important to take the time to really understand each player's deficiencies and set up a program that will put everyone on the right track. (See Part 2 for more in-depth information on developing a young hitter.)

During one particular season I had a player who had a tremendous uppercut and was having trouble hitting off the batting machine at 40 miles an hour. At practice, I noticed that he kept his hands low and that his shoulder was down, a combination that made it almost impossible for him to make contact with the ball. I showed the player and the rest of the team how to bring the hands parallel to the shoulder, which eliminated shoulder drop and uppercutting. I then devised a routine in which they hit off a tee from high in the strike zone, to get the feel of a level swing. Then we worked on a bat knob-to-ball exercise (see page 73) to practice the most efficient use of a swing.

Before I knew it, all of the players were hitting off the batting machine consistently. Working on one

Hitting a ball off a high tee can help a player develop a level swing.

player's weakness had helped everyone improve, and by continuing the process they all improved further. Repetitive exercises are part of a strong program, and young players won't mind them when they see they're succeeding.

Another key part of a strong program is speaking to the team right after every game. Young players often forget fundamentals taught during practice and attempted during games, so it's important to immediately point out situations in which technique was critical in executing an at-bat or a play in the field. Post-game discussion isn't the time to correct young players on what they did wrong but to discuss plays that exemplified good fundamentals and hustle. Doing so will reinforce positive thinking and encourage players to speak up and try even harder.

At the beginning of each practice, also discuss what you covered in the previous practice, to reinforce learning and to discover what the team should work on next. Ask open-ended questions to ensure that concepts were understood and absorbed. Target techniques or concepts the kids are struggling with and spend time on drills that will make them successful. At the end of each practice, make sure the players grasped the drills and that each player successfully completed each drill at least once. As kids master skills, they will want to learn more.

Regardless, continue working on skill fundamentals. You will probably be pressured by players, parents, and, sometimes, even your assistant coaches to introduce more complex concepts before the basics have been mastered. Introducing new concepts that players are not prepared for can lead to failure or a false sense of readiness. Making one long hit or a one-handed grab does not mean that a player is ready to move on. What separates a great player from an average one is that the great player refines his or her skills.

Successful Experience

CHAPTER 3

Managing the Basics: Practice Plans, Checklists, Conditioning, and Scorekeeping

Developing players' hitting and fielding skills is keys to team success. But to make that happen, you need to develop practice plans and task checklists, condition your players, and learn the intricacies of scorekeeping.

Developing a Season Practice Plan and Individual Practice Sessions

How well you conduct practice sessions and prepare your players for competition will greatly affect not only your players' enjoyment and success throughout the season but yours as well. The following pointers should help you put together an overall practice plan and individual practice sessions that promote teamwork and learning as well as fun.

Before the season begins, sit down with your coaching staff to map out a season practice plan that will work for them and for parents. I recommend using an Excel spreadsheet to number your practices and to put your game dates on the calendar. Numbering your practices will make it easy for parents and coaches to follow along and will enable you and your coaching staff to refer quickly to each practice. For each practice, note its purpose, the main skills to be covered, and the drills to be used.

As you put together individual practice plans (see the example below), be sure to include some diversity in your drill selection. Also step up the drill difficulty as the season progresses and players improve. Because one of the goals of practices is to replicate a game environment, be sure to include game-like drills. This will help players become more

Important Practice Points

1. Practice as a team, not as individuals.
2. Start each practice by letting your players and coaches know the agenda.
3. Establish a practice routine so players and coaches know what to expect.
4. Have coaches run the drills and be in charge of rotating players.
5. Take scheduled breaks to keep players fresh and focused.
6. When correcting mistakes, focus on giving positive feedback.
7. Follow the "80-20" rule: demonstrate 80% of the time and speak 20% of the time.
8. Enforce the rule that players who consistently miss practice do not play in games.
9. Show respect and compassion at all times.

comfortable on game days and also help them develop the physical and mental skills needed to play in a game.

As you put together practices, remember that this age group has had little to no exposure to baseball and, if they have, many kids will have forgotten what they learned in previous seasons. Those who have had a couple of years of experience will say that they already know a certain drill and don't need to practice it. Make sure they understand that even big leaguers practice throughout their careers to keep their skills sharp.

Creating a season practice plan can be challenging, so don't be afraid to ask current or previous coaches to help you draft one. Also develop some back-up drills or activities that you can switch to, or decide to go back to practicing a more elemental

skill, if you find that a particular practice plan doesn't work.

Understanding the Game Rules

Knowing the rules of the game is as important as teaching them—you can't teach well without a thorough understanding of how the game is played. The following section provides a basic overview of the different developmental divisions and the rules that apply to each, but because different leagues may follow slightly different rules, it's important for you and interested parents to talk with officials about the rules for your particular league. In all games, the home team bats second, after the visiting team, and is generally the team whose field is used. In leagues in which

---

Sample Practice Plan, Ages 4 to 6

Total Practice Time: 65 Minutes

1. **Five minutes: all players run the bases three times**
   - Players must touch all bases or start over again
   - No player is to pass another
   - At the end of the run players yell, "First base is the only base you can run past!"
2. **Five minutes: stretching** (two players take turns leading, 20 movements per set)
   - Two sets of jumping jacks
   - Two sets of toe touches
   - Two sets of arm circles
   - Two sets of hip rotations with hands on hips
3. **Five minutes: define the day's plan**
   - Describe the drills
   - Break players into groups to be led by the coach or volunteers
4. **Thirty minutes: practice in stations** (10 minutes at each)
   - Hit off the tee: 3-5 players
   - Soft toss pitching to players: 3-5 players

- Stance and swing fundamentals: 3-5 players
Note: You can substitute other age-appropriate hitting drills from Chapter 8.
5. **Fifteen minutes: play instructional game**
   - One player hits off the tee
   - Six players are in the field, with no catcher or outfielders
   - On the third hit the player runs to first
   - Fielders try to get batter out, fielders rotate positions
   - Batters waiting to hit, practice with coach
   - Everyone bats once
6. **Five minutes: players run bases for speed and review**
   - All players run bases one time
   - Review the practice
   - Remind parents of the next practice/game and place
   - Recognize everyone for a job well done

Sample Practice Plan, Ages 7 to 10

Total Practice Time: 1 Hour and 25 Minutes

1. **Ten minutes: cardio warm-up** (two players take turns leading, 30 movements per set)
   - All players run around the field one time
   - Three sets of jumping jacks
   - Jogging in place with high knees
   - Arm stretches with elbows behind head
   - Three sets of hamstring and toe touches
   - Three sets of arm circles
   - Three sets of hip rotations with hands on hips
2. **Ten minutes: run bases twice, do relay drill**
   - All players must touch all bases or start over
   - No player is to pass another
   - After all players run the bases, one player runs to first base, rounds the bag, goes back to first, and yells, "Go!"; the next player repeats the drill
3. **Five minutes: define the day's plan**
   - Describe drills
   - Break players into groups to be led by the coach or parent volunteers
4. **Thirty minutes: practice in stations** (10 minutes at each)
   - Hit off the tee: 3-5 players
   - Soft toss pitching: 3-5 players
   - Coach pitches: 3-5 players (players not hitting should play infield
   Note: You can substitute other age-appropriate hitting drills from Chapter 8.
5. **Twenty-five minutes: play instructional game**
   - Coach pitches or batter hits from batting machine
   - Coaches monitor fielding, running, and hitting
   - Nine players are in the field, one at each position with an extra outfielder, no catcher
   - On the fifth hit the player runs to first
   - The fielder tries to get the batter out; if the batter is safe, he or she stays on base and game rules apply
   - Fielders rotate positions until their turn at bat
   - Everyone bats once
6. **Five minutes: run bases for speed and review**
   - All players run bases one time
   - Review the practice
   - Remind parents of the next practice/game and location
   - Recognize everyone for a job well done

all teams use the same field, league officials should predetermine the home team. In most leagues, the home team takes care of preparing the field and the visiting team puts equipment away.

Tee-Ball and Coach Pitch Divisions

The purpose of these divisions is to teach players the fundamentals of baseball and to have a good time. Players at this level are usually having their first expe-rience with organized baseball, so it's important that managers and coaches make it positive and fun. Be-cause all players are not at the same skill level, it is also important that everyone receive the same encour-agement, regardless of the outcome of a play. To keep it fun and to prevent exhaustion, it's best to keep games under an hour and a half.

The game rules are:

1. Games are three innings with no outs

Here the rules are:

1. The pitching machine is controlled by the manager of the team that is batting.

2. The pitching machine is set to throw strikes, at approximately 40 miles per hour.

3. Each batter receives five hittable pitches.

4. Six innings are played.

5. There are three outs per inning or players can bat through the lineup once, then switch teams.

6. There are no errors.

7. Runners can take extra bases when a clean hit goes into the outfield (discuss the exact terms of this with the opposing coach).

8. Players should not play more than two innings at the same position.

9. The batting lineup should be rotated every game.

recorded—when the last batter bats, the inning is over.

2. For coach-pitched games, each player receives up to seven hittable pitches.

3. Every player plays.

4. No score is kept.

5. Player positions are rotated each inning and the batting order is rotated each game.

Machine Pitch Division

At this level the same fundamental philosophy applies—players need to have an enjoyable experience while they continue learning baseball fundamentals.

10. All players bat and play the field.

11. All players should try to play catcher.

Player Pitch Division

Though players pitch to each other in this division, it is still a developmental division with the focus on refining hitting and fielding techniques. However, pitching, bunting, and base-stealing fundamentals are now added to the mix. Also, scores are kept as well as batting averages. Each team pitches, with an umpire calling balls and strikes. In this division, official Little League rules apply.

Here the rules are:

1. Player pitches to opposing batter.

2. Balls and strikes are kept by umpire.

3. Six innings are played.

4. There are three outs per inning then the next team bats.

Scoring Examples

Ryan, the left fielder (7) is the first batter. The count goes to three balls, one strike, and then the batter hits a double (2B). He later scores when the second batter singles.

Loucks, the catcher (2), with a count of one ball, two strikes, hits a single (1B) to score the left fielder. The catcher is credited with a run batted in (RBI) with the number 1 in his RBI box.

Vieira, the first baseman (3) hits the first pitch but flies out to center field for the first out. The out is shown by a circled number.

Allen, the third baseman (5) strikes out by swinging on three straight pitches. The strikeout is shown with a K in the batter box and the second out of the inning is shown with a circled 2.

Lucas, the center fielder (8), with a count of one ball, hits a grounder to the third baseman, who throws to first for the third out of the inning.

   The totals for the inning are: one run, two hits, no errors, and one runner left on base. The left fielder is credited with scoring the run.

NO.	LINE UP	POS	1	
3	¹ RYAN	7	2B	
16	² LOUCKS	2	1B	
14	³ VIEIRA	3	F-8 ①	
9	⁴ ALLEN	6	Ks ②	
11	⁵ LUCAS	8	5-3 ③	
5	⁶ MARK	4	X	

TOTALS	RUNS			1
	H	E	LOB	2 0 1 1

Numbering:

Pitcher = 1
Catcher = 2
First base = 3
Second base = 4
Third base = 5
Shortstop = 6
Left field = 7
Center field = 8
Right field = 9
Additional outfielder = 10

Abbreviations:

Balk = BK
Base on balls = BB
Bunt = B
Double play = DP
Error = E
Fielder's choice = FC
Fly-out = F
Foul fly-out = FF
Hit by pitch = HP

Home run = HR
Intentional walk = IW
One-base hit = 1B
Out stealing = OS
Passed ball = PB
Run batted in = RBI
Run scored = R
Sacrifice = SAC
Stolen base = SB

Strikeout = K
Three-base hit = 3B
Triple play = TP
Two-base hit = 2B
Wild pitch = WP

5. Scoring is kept and recorded. (There is a scoring limit per inning in most leagues.)

6. Runner can advance a base at own risk while ball is in play.

7. Players can tag-up on a caught fly ball, steal, and bunt.

8. Players rotated to different playing positions.

9. Pitches per game and number of days pitched limits are enforced.

10. All players bat and play field.

Establishing the Batting Order

Before the start of each game, the coach or manager of each team must submit a batting order to the umpire in charge. A copy of the batting order must also be given to the scorekeeper and the opposing coach. The batting order lists the name and uniform number of each player at his or her position in the lineup (all players should bat). The batting order list should also include the names of available substitutes. Baseball rules state that only starting players can reenter the game after a substitute has replaced them, but check with league officials for specific rules regarding substitutions.

Keeping Score

Keeping score is an important part of keeping track of the game and making sure all players bat and play the proper positions. It also shows you and your staff how your hitters are doing.

Using a scorebook is not difficult once you know the numbering system and the appropriate abbreviations. Several examples of scoring are given at left.

How to Score

At-Bats—Batters are charged with an official time at bat every time they are up, except when they receive a base on balls (BB), are hit by a pitch (HP), advance runners with a sacrifice bunt (SAC-B), score a runner with a sacrifice fly (SAC-F), or are given first base because of catcher interference.

Hits—Credit batters with a base hit when: they safely reach first base or beyond on a fair ball hit cleanly through the infield or to the outfield, landing untouched; when they reach base safely on a ball hit so slowly or so hard or that takes a bad bounce that makes it impossible, in your judgment, to field it with normal effort in time to make the out; and when they hit a fair ball that is not touched by a fielder but hits an umpire or a runner.

How to Figure Batting Averages—To determine a player's batting average, divide the total number of base hits he or she has by his or her total official times at bat.

PART 2

Teaching Hitting Fundamentals

In this section of the book you'll find more in-depth information about how to help players aged four to ten develop hitting skills. Included are pointers on how to grip the bat, how to stand correctly, and how to swing and release. Both the physical and mental aspects of hitting well are covered.

CHAPTER 4

Bat to Hand Method

Line up knuckles—palms line up vertically.

Place bat handle on the fingers of the batter's open hands.

Gripping the Bat

One of the fundamental elements of hitting a baseball well is holding the bat properly. Although players use additional parts of their body to carry out a good swing, the hands directly connect with the bat and are the foundation of a smooth, controlled, repeatable swing. The first step in developing young hitters, then, is to teach them how to hold the bat properly. The following "Bat to Hand" exercise does just that. (See photos of each step below.) I encourage you to have players go through the exercise before every hitting practice.

To start, lay the handle of the bat across the fingers of both of the player's open hands, with the pinkie of one hand touching the index finger of the other hand. Then have the player close his or her hands around the handle. The big knuckles of both hands should line up vertically. To see if the player is holding the bat correctly, have the child point his or her index fingers out. Both fingers should point parallel to one another. If players are uncomfortable aligning their knuckles, have them grab a pen or pencil to get the feel and to concentrate on hand positioning rather than swinging.

Once players understand how to position their fingers to grip the bat, make sure they do not hold it too tightly—a light but firm grip keeps the muscles of the fingers, hands, wrist, forearms, and shoulders loose, and loose muscles are fast muscles that give players the best chance of quickly releasing the bat to the ball. Most young players like to strangle the bat, however, so pay special attention that their grip allows them to move their wrists. Also remind young players not to hold the bat back in the palm of their hands. Gripping in this way inhibits wrist rotation during the swing and robs the hitter of speed and power.

Player closes hands gently but firmly.

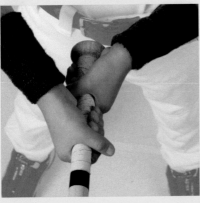

Player points index fingers out so they are parallel.

Player brings fingers back into position, with flexible wrists.

CHAPTER 5

Aligning the feet

The player steps into the batter's box and should be able to touch the outside edge of the plate with the end of the bat. This will give the hitter complete plate coverage.

Developing the Correct Stance

With the proper grip in place, the next thing to do is to teach young hitters how to stand and address the ball. Standing correctly gives children the best chance of transferring their weight through their hips, centering the ball on the bat, and making contact, all in the short amount of time they have to react. It also allows hitters to stay balanced and freely stride out with their front foot after a hit.

The stance I teach below is called the neutral stance. I don't recommend teaching the two other stances, the closed stance and the open stance, to players between the ages of four and ten because they can encourage bad habits and can make it more difficult to teach and learn baseball fundamentals. The open stance and the closed stance should be taught only to more established players who are dealing with more advanced pitching techniques. The neutral stance gives young players the best possibility for success.

Aligning the Feet

While stepping up to the plate sounds simple, it is the biggest way for a young player to get himself or herself into trouble. Many young hitters stand on the plate or outside the batter's box, making it difficult for them to see the ball and make solid contact with it and more likely that they'll get hit with it. Although young play-

The player makes a mark where the knob of the bat ends once he has found plate coverage.

The player draws a line parallel to the plate at this mark where his feet will be.

The player places his toes parallel to the line he has drawn.

Stance

ers will probably begin by playing tee ball, with no one pitching to them, they'll eventually face pitchers and will need to know how to properly meet the ball. Showing them the right way early on will prevent them from falling into bad hitting habits.

Before beginning to instruct your players, and before every practice and game, make sure the batter's box is level and free of debris. Then teach your team the following steps and have each player carry them out at every at-bat.

1. The player steps into the batter's box and should be able to touch the outside edge of the plate with the end of the bat. This will give the hitter complete plate coverage.

2. The player makes a mark where the knob of the bat ends once he has found plate coverage.

3. The player draws a line parallel to the plate at this mark where his feet will be.

4. The player places his toes parallel to the line he has drawn.

Aligning the Shoulders

Some coaches instruct their players to keep their back elbow up, but this is not correct. Holding the back elbow up could change the swing plane, which can

A player's feet should turn in just slightly, "pigeon toed," and are spread a little more than the width of the player's shoulders with the knees slightly bent and inside the feet.

cause the bat to be misaligned and affect how quickly the player can swing the bat.

The proper way for players to align their shoulders is with the back shoulder level with the front. The forearms and hands should form an upside-down "V" and stay fairly close to the body.

This position allows players to move the bat along the easiest and quickest route to the ball.

Finding Balance

A proper stance enables young hitters not only to see the ball better but to take advantage of the correct mechanics of the swing—it enables the eyes and the hands to work well together. Unnecessary, unbal-

The player's forearms form an upside down "V."

anced movement, especially of the hitter's head, will inhibit the player from tracking the plane of the ball.

A balanced (neutral) stance for young players requires that both feet turn in just slightly, "pigeon toed," and are spread a little more than the width of the player's shoulders. The hitter stands on the balls of the feet, not flat-footed, with the knees slightly bent and inside the feet. To test if players are standing correctly, gently push them in the chest. If you knock them off balance, you know they were not standing on the balls of their feet. Also test from the back. If players fall forward, you know they were standing on their toes, which is too far forward.

Test each player to see how he or she is standing. Kids love this drill, and they may want to try it on you too. Just make sure you hold the exercise in a safe area so that no one—including you—gets hurt if they fall.

Once kids can find the right position, increase their balance by having them bend their knees a bit more, just to the point where they would be comfortable sitting on their bat or a stool. If they can't find this position, have them close their eyes and put their hands on their hips as they bend their knees. Once they look and feel balanced, have them open their eyes. Players should feel light footed and ready to react.

Putting It All Together

When players know how to hold the bat and get into a balanced stance, have them put the two together by checking elements off on a mental checklist. Have them do this before they take a swing.

First, they should check their feet, which should be slightly pigeon-toed. Next, they should check their grip, which should be relaxed but firm, with the right hand on top for left-handed hitters and the left hand on top for right-handed hitters. Third, they should check their head, arms, and bat placement. Their head should face the pitcher's mound and they should look out over the front shoulder, with both eyes on the target. The bat should rest slightly above the back shoulder, with elbows slightly raised and held close to the body.

During practice and during games, make sure even the youngest players take the time to set them-

selves up for a quality swing. One good swing will put the ball in play, whereas many poor swings will take much more time and effort and have a greater probability of failure. When coaching young hitters, remind them that the best major league hitters prepare for their at-bats and control the tempo of the game.

Stance

CHAPTER 6

Developing an Effective Swing

To hit a baseball well, players need to combine mental readiness with physical readiness. But at this age, children shouldn't be expected to do much in-depth thinking regarding their times at bat. Many young players can barely find their way to the plate let alone give any thought to what they are going to do once they get there. However, having the right frame of mind—being happy, excited, and confident—as well as being physically prepared will help youngsters make the best of their times at the plate.

Getting Hitters Ready

To be mentally and physically ready to hit the ball, players should take the following steps:

1. The night before a game, young hitters should pack their bat, gloves, helmet, cleats, and good luck charm if they have one. This will get them thinking positively about hitting the ball the next day.

2. Have players arrive early enough before the game to warm up. Children need time to make the transition from one activity to another. Have them stretch out and swing the bat.

3. Before the game starts, have the players listen to you relate the batting order. This will help them relax and think about getting ready for their turn at the plate.

4. Before their time at bat, have players spend time in the on-deck circle, away from distractions, getting comfortable with their swing and concentrating on making solid contact with the ball. Have them find red stitches on the ball being pitched to hitter at bat.

5. When their turn at bat arrives, have young hitters put on their game face. Also have them go through their mental positioning checklist (see page 48).

6. When they feel comfortable and ready, remind them that their single goal is to hit the ball.

After their turn at bat, young hitters should concentrate on the positive things about it. Encourage them to remember the feel of a good swing or the base hit that they made.

Choosing the Right Bat

When choosing a bat, most young hitters grab whatever is available or one they like the looks of, or parents go out and buy them an expensive one—which isn't much better than a moderately priced bat. The most important part of choosing a bat is to pick one that the player can handle well and is the right weight and size. Many times I've seen young hitters lugging heavy, long bats in the hope that these bats will give them a better chance of making contact with the ball, just the way many of us think that a bigger tennis racket or bigger driver will help us hit the ball better. But what is actually needed is a better swing and lots of practice.

To help children choose the right bat, which will be their best friend, watch them swing the bat to see if they can both start and stop their swing with control and balance. Next have them take the bat in their dominant hand at the very end of the handle and hold the bat straight out from their body parallel to the ground. They should be able to keep their arm completely straight, without dropping the barrel or straining their arm, for about 15 seconds. If children have trouble holding the bat, tell them to think about some-

An Effective Swing

thing lighter—a light bat will give them better speed and more control. As far as length goes, a longer bat is better than a short one, within reason. A good rule of thumb is to buy a bat that is about one or two inches longer than what might be appropriate for that hitter's height and age. Any local sporting goods store should be able to help determine what is right. Using a slightly longer bat lets hitters grow into the bat without hindering their development. They can choke up on the bat especially if it is light and manageable.

Metal versus Wood Bats

The de facto bat standard is an aluminum or a composite bat because of these bats' durability. Metal bats are more expensive than wood bats, though, and I believe that young hitters get a better feel for the ball using a wood bat. Whichever type batters choose, avoid having them switch to a different type during the season. Both types of bats have a distinctive feel, and switching from one to the other could affect a hitter's swing. If batters change mid-season from a metal bat, they may think that something is wrong with their swing.

Putting the Swing in Motion

The proper grip and stance will maximize the swing motion. When these three elements come together correctly, they result in an automatic grip, stance, and swing movement that is not only beautiful to look at but makes hitting the ball easier.

To develop a quality swing, a young hitter's muscles should be relaxed, not tense. When they're relaxed, muscles can sync up with the hitter's brain to properly perform the swing command. They also react more quickly and increase the probability of players centering the ball on the bat.

Before the Swing

Before players address the ball, they need to go through a pre-swing routine to increase their concentration and get ready to connect with the ball. The pre-swing drill is critical to hitting well. Have your players practice it repeatedly until it's second nature to them and ingrained in their muscle memory.

Have players start by making small, tight semicircular motions with the bat and rhythmically shifting their upper body. Their feet should be stationary, but they should be able to feel their weight shifting slightly from the inside of one foot to the other.

Next, when the ball is about to be delivered (whether from a tee, another player, or the coach), players should bring their body weight back in one efficient movement. Their body should feel balanced, and their weight should stay on the inside of the rear foot, with the toe of the front foot lifting just slightly toward the target. This is called the load position. Once in the load position, hitters are ready to release the energy in their swing.

Releasing the Swing

Players should take these steps to properly release their swing:

1. *Align feet and grip.* Once in the batter's box player should check their grip and make sure they have a balanced stance a little wider than the shoulders with feet parallel to the plate.

2. *Get in the neutral position.* Bat should be raised to ready position with eyes fixed on the target. Shoulders should be even. Forearms should beclose to the body in an inverted "V". Knees should be bent with weight balanced on the inside of the heels.

3. *Load body weight to back foot.* Head stays still. Body weight shifts back with pressure on inside back foot. The front heel should be stable or slightly raised.

4. *Rotate hips for power.* Hips rotate while head stays still. Hands bring bat to contact—"knob to ball." Top hand comes down bringing barrel down to the ball. Body weight is shifted back to center. Back foot and knee transfer power to a firm front side of the body.

5. *Hitting through the batting zone.* Eyes should be on target with head level. Bat contact is made by keeping hands inside of the ball. Power is captured by front leg with front foot firmly planted.

(continued on page 60)

The following pages illustrate the process of putting the swing in motion

1. Align feet and grip

Clear mind— think hitting

Check grip

Balanced stance wider than shoulders

Knees slightly bent

Weight on inside of rear foot

Feet parallel to plate

An Effective Swing

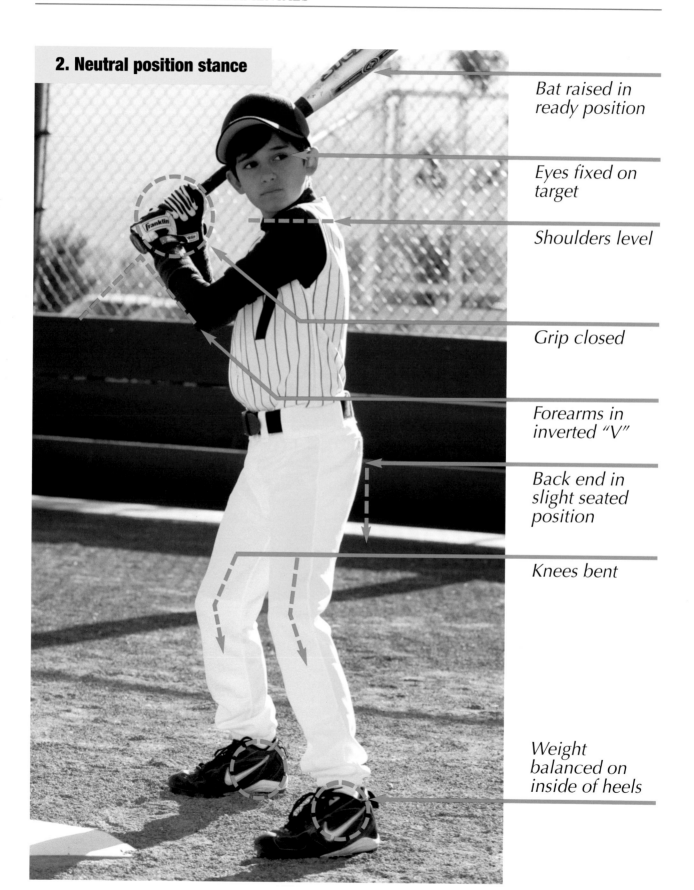

2. Neutral position stance

Bat raised in ready position

Eyes fixed on target

Shoulders level

Grip closed

Forearms in inverted "V"

Back end in slight seated position

Knees bent

Weight balanced on inside of heels

3. Load body weight to back foot

Eyes level—
head still

Shoulders
parallel

Hands come
down to target

Shift body
weight back

Pressure on
inside of foot

Front heel
stable or
slightly raised

4. Rotate hips for power

Eyes on target

Shoulders stay closed—head stays still

Hands bring knob to ball to position for contact

Shift body weight back to center

Hips open up and rotate

Back foot and knee rotate to transfer power

Front foot now takes weight for power

5. Hitting through the batting zone

Eyes on target—head level

Bat contact level with extension through the hitting zone

Power is captured in front leg with front foot firmly planted

Rotation of rear foot is finished

An Effective Swing

6. The follow-through

Eyes stay on target after contact—head stays level and still

Accelerating through ball generating power

Full hip extension

Front leg releasing stored power

Both feet still firmly planted

7. Finish strong

Swing bat down behind shoulders

Eyes still on target after contact—head stays level and still

Hips finish at full extension

Front leg has released power

Front foot still planted as power is released

An Effective Swing

6. *The follow-through.* Eyes stay at contact point with head still. Player accelerates through the ball generating power. Full hip extension with belly button facing target. Front leg and foot still firmly planted releasing stored power.

7. *Finishing strong.* Swing ends with bat behind shoulders. Eyes are still on point of contact with hips finishing at full extension. Front leg and foot finish releasing power. Front foot is still planted.

The Load Process

The swing actually starts when players load body weight to their back foot. This device should become a mental trigger for players to release their swing's energy. For most young hitters, just lifting the front heel should be more than enough to get the swing going; you shouldn't encourage players to lift their foot off the ground, and if they do they shouldn't move it more than three to six inches, directly toward the target. Taking a stride of more than six inches can break apart the entire routine.

Players should bring their front foot down on the inside of the ball of the foot, turned a little inside, "pigeon-toe" style. Their front leg and foot should be centered and straight to the ball; even a small turn left or right opens up the hips and front shoulder, causing a player to miss or foul off a pitch. Once the front foot is planted, it should stay there, feeling light to players but in place. If players step forward too hard, they can lose the leverage generated from the pre-swing. (When hitters are more mature, they can work on going with the

Players should bring their front foot down on the inside of the ball of the foot, staying closed, "pigeon-toe" style, their front leg centered and straight to the ball.

"Squashing the Bug"

The heel of the rear foot should be lifted; the player pivots onto the ball of the rear foot and pushes hard.

pitch, which involves manipulating the hips and shoulders to place the ball.) However, they must transfer their weight so they don't hit from a dead stop.

A good indication that the foot is coming down correctly is that players are hitting hard line drives that go through the center of the diamond. A lot of foul balls means that the opposite is happening. When players step in the wrong direction, their shoulders open up and their plate coverage is reduced, because they've committed their body to one direction. If you find that young hitters hit the ball weakly, with foul balls going far to the left or right, remind them to keep their front foot planted and their shoulder in. You will be amazed at how quickly this will have them making solid contact with the ball.

Rotating the Feet, Legs, and Hips ("Squashing the Bug")

Rotating the rear foot, lifting up the heel, and putting pressure on the ball of the foot transfers body weight to the hips. It also generates energy that travels like an electrical current down the rear leg and

foot, releasing power and profoundly affecting a swing. Many first-time batting instructors believe that the legs generate the swing's power when it is actually the turning of the back foot, which triggers hip rotation. This foot manipulation, which I call "Squashing the Bug," is an easy skill to teach and one young hitters love to practice.

A great way to teach this movement is to have players take their pre-swing stance holding a pencil instead of a bat. As they get ready to take a slow-motion swing, say, "Squash the bug!" Show them how to turn their back foot and push hard on the ball of their foot. Not only do they have fun doing it, but they learn the motion quickly.

Tell your young hitters that learning to correctly move their feet and hips means hits! This should stimulate them to use their lower body muscles to put power in their swing.

Keeping the Front of the Body Steady

When hitters lift their front foot and then move their weight from back to front while rotating their hips, extreme pressure is put on the front of the body. Hitters need to trap and control this energy for their swing, which they do by keeping the front of their body steady and by planting their front leg, which captures the weight from the rear foot and hip.

A good mental image for hitters to have is that their feet are cemented in a solid front position. They can't move their feet either forward or backward. However, they can rotate their hips and upper body, enabling them to transfer movement forward during their swing. The more firmly planted the front of their body is, the better they'll be able to capture the full power of their swing.

As the upper body comes forward, many young hitters throw their front shoulder out too early, thinking

Hitters control the energy for their swing by keeping the front of their body steady.

they are creating additional leverage. This is incorrect. Instead, teach players to rest their chin on their front shoulder. If their head stays steady, their body will rotate well and their front shoulder will not pull away.

Using the Hands Efficiently

Why did I spend so much time on proper feet, hip, and shoulder positioning? So that players' hands will be in the right position to work more effectively and efficiently with the bat—the lower body and the hands work together. Many young players think they would hit the ball better if they had quicker bat speed, but the real problem is usually wasted hand movement.

Players' hands need to stay above and inside the baseball at all times. If the hands get away from the body or drop below the ball, the swing becomes slow and loopy. The proper swing path is downward or level to the ball and should be short to the ball. At contact, the barrel should be above the hands.

Here are the steps players should take to use their hands efficiently during a swing:

1. The bottom hand takes the knob of the bat to the ball. The top hand then brings the barrel "down" to the ball.

2. At the point of contact, the barrel of the bat should be above the hands. The top hand palm is up and the bottom hand palm is down.

3. Once the players make contact with the ball, they should extend the barrel through the ball until the arms are fully extended.

4. Players should then roll their wrists into the follow-through, up and over their front shoulder and back.

As you can see, the two hands work together. The top hand is stronger, but the bottom hand acts as the guide, giving direction and support to the dominant hand. Often you will see players release their top hand during or right after contact, but I don't recommend this. I believe batters generate more power by controlling the bat with both hands. Certainly any player who weighs less than 125 pounds needs to hold the bat with both hands, both for generating as much power as possible as well as for preventing the bat from flying off.

Finishing the Swing

Once players have made solid contact with the ball, they need to follow through to get every bit of distance possible. When instructing your players, tell them that bat-to-ball contact slows down the swing, so they need to actually accelerate their swing and

Hand Transition

The bottom hand takes the knob of the bat to the ball. The top hand then brings the barrel "down" to the ball.

At the point of contact, the top hand palm is up and the bottom hand palm is down.

Once the players make contact with the ball, they should extend the barrel through the ball until the arms are fully extended.

Players should then roll their wrists into the follow-through, up and over their front shoulder and back.

not stop until the bat is over their shoulder and behind their back, to increase bat speed and give them better control. The follow-through does not come naturally, so young hitters will need to practice it routinely.

Although the swing is short to the ball, it is long through the hit and follow-through. The longer the bat stays in the hitting zone, the better success the player will have. At the furthest extension, the barrel of the bat should be pointed at the pitcher or pitching machine—the difference between a ground ball and a line drive to the outfield is extension.

An Effective Swing

CHAPTER 7

Turning a Good Swing into Base Hits

If all pitches were thrown down the middle of the plate, all at the same height, hitters could swing on the exact same swing plane every time and hit the ball. This, of course, doesn't happen in Little League (or anywhere else), especially when coaches and young children are pitching. Because of the unpredictability of pitches, hitting the baseball is the single most difficult task for players to master.

Meeting the Ball Directly

To hit the baseball, young players must have a swing that is repeatable and is guided by line of sight to point of contact. Tracking the ball's movement is crucial, because not only does a ball travel fast but it travels downward after leaving the pitcher's hand or the pitching machine's mouth.

Young players need to adjust to the falling flight of the ball and meet the ball on a downward plane. Their swing should match the path of the traveling baseball as closely as possible.

Keeping Eyes on the Ball

Good hitters keep their eyes on the ball and meet the ball at the last moment square on the sweet spot. If you ingrain in players' heads the old baseball saying "See the ball, hit the ball," that concept will help them succeed.

But teaching young hitters to keep their eyes fixed on an object for any length of time can be very challenging. Usually they can concentrate on an object for not more than a few seconds. To increase concentration, have players practice this drill. Have them start

by focusing on the lettering on the pitcher's cap—they need a starting point to work from. As the pitcher brings his or her arm forward to throw the ball, hitters should move their eyes from the cap to the pitcher's hand through the point of release. Then they should follow the ball all the way to the point of contact. They should keep their eyes glued to the ball at all times, with their head down and straight, chin touching chest. By keeping their chin on their chest, they'll keep their head in line with their shoulder and synchronize with their back and triceps muscles, which

The hitter should first focus on the pitcher's cap. As the pitcher brings his or her arm forward to throw the ball, hitters should move their eyes from the cap to the pitcher's hand until he releases the ball.

Eyes on the Ball

will make their swing more compact, accurate, and powerful.

An exercise I learned at a Little League coaching clinic may help players at the older end of the spectrum increase their concentration and fine-tune muscle strength. Players stare at the largest of five baseballs pictured on a chart for as long as possible without blinking. Then they rest their eyes a few moments and repeat the exercise 10 more times. The next day they repeat it 10 more times staring at the second-largest ball, and so on. The thought is that if hitters concentrate on objects smaller than a normal-sized baseball for a period longer than it takes for a pitch to cross the plate, the game baseball will seem larger and more in focus.

During practices and games, make sure players focus on a target on the pitcher's mound or the tee. Putting a half-inch dot on baseballs you use for practices will help hitters improve their timing and make the swing plane adjustment.

Letting the Ball Come to You

Many young hitters tend to move toward the ball, or what I call "fall off the cliff," before they're ready to swing—they don't wait for the ball to come to them because they're anxious to make contact, and this state of mind causes them to lunge at the ball and release energy before contact. But good hitters are relaxed and have the discipline to let the ball come to them, and even the youngest hitters can learn to do this.

The exercise that follows can help players of all ages learn to wait for the ball to come to them. The drill requires that a pitcher lob overhand or underhand tosses to players from 30 feet away. I recommend using an L-screen if hitters are older than six.

1. Draw half-inch red or blue dots on 10 of 20 baseballs.

2. Ask hitters to swing at only the dotted balls, letting the unmarked balls go by.

By concentrating on the ball, hitters swing only at the 10 balls marked with dots out of 20 balls.

Avoiding a Bad Pitch

By turning their front shoulder and body inward toward the catcher, it ensures that, if they are hit, it will be in the least vulnerable parts of the body.

3. Have them hold the load position (see page 60 for a reminder) in the batter's box until the ball reaches the plate.

4. Have hitters swing as the first ball crosses the plate, not before.

5. Have each player complete the drill by swinging at only the 10 of 20 baseballs that have dots.

Avoiding Being Hit

It's perfectly normal for developing hitters to be afraid of being hit by a baseball. Many children stand at the plate more concerned about being hit by a pitch than about carrying out the proper swing and getting a hit. Learning to track the ball will give them confidence that they can move out of the way if necessary and that, in most cases, they won't be hit, so it's important for them to work on the exercises in "Keeping Eyes on the Ball," above. Knowing how to protect themselves

will also help to give them peace of mind and let them concentrate on hitting.

If players think they are about to be hit by a pitch, they should turn their front shoulder and body inward toward the catcher. Turning in this way ensures that, if they are hit, it will be in the least vulnerable parts of the body—the back, buttocks, or back of the legs.

An exercise that should help reduce the fear of being hit is to actually throw soft, easy pitches at the players after you've taught them to turn toward the catcher. Have hitters stand at the plate one at a time and tell them that you are going to attempt to hit them. Throw several—but not all of—your pitches at the hitter, being sure to throw slowly and easily with a soft rubber ball. Your hitters will find out that most of the time they can avoid being hit—the most important thing—as well as gain confidence that they can protect themselves and lessen the blow when they are hit.

Eyes on the Ball

PART 3

Practice Drills

In this section, you'll find 18 exercises that will help develop players' motor skills as well as increase confidence and comfort levels and players' possibilities for success. Choose the drills that best suit your team's needs, and remember not to run drills that are too difficult for the age group to master. On the other hand, don't be afraid to expose even the youngest players to a variety of drills.

CHAPTER 8

Perfect Practice Makes Perfect—Hitting Drills

In this chapter I offer a wide range of basic hitting drills that both develop skills and are fun to do. The drills are all appropriate for children aged four to ten. Because I believe that books about baseball try to cover too much territory, I don't include more advanced drills for more advanced players.

Each drill includes a description, the drill's goal, any needed equipment, how to run the drill, and the key to coaching the exercise. I also suggest ideas for making the drills even more fun.

Drill 1. Batter Warm-up Exercises (ages 4-10)

Description: Preparing the arms, legs, and torso for batting.

Goal: To get batters warm and loose for productive batting-drill sessions.

Equipment: Bats

Coaching Key: Be certain players have enough space to execute the warm-up exercises and that they move slowly, holding the bat firmly at all times.

How to Run Them:

The Over-the-Head Bat Twirl
Batters raise their bat over their head and gently rotate their wrists 360 degrees. They perform the exercise 10 times clockwise and 10 times counter-clockwise.

The Bat-Behind-the-Head Pull
Batters put their bat in their right hand and bring it back behind their head with their left hand, with the left hand gently pulling down and the right hand staying in place. Have players reverse their hands and repeat the drill, continuing for 30 seconds.

Trunk Twist
Batters put their bat behind their back horizontally, through their locked elbows, while standing in the hitting position. Then they rotate their body 180 degrees five times, turning slowly.

(continued)

Drills

Drill 1. Batter Warm-up Exercises (continued)

Toe Touches with the Bat

Batters hold their bat horizontally with both hands and slowly touch their toes with it, holding for five seconds. After standing back up, they repeat the exercise.

Practice Swings

Batters assume the proper batting stance and take five forceful swings, watching their form.

Extra Fun: Each time a player masters an exercise, give him or her a helmet sticker.

Wrist Rotation

Batters take their bat in their right hand with a firm grip and gently rotate their wrist five times. Then they repeat the drill with their left hand.

Drill 2. Hip Rotation Drill (ages 4-10)

Description: Players track the ball in the proper stance.

Goal: To develop muscle memory using leg drive and hip, torso, and abdominal (core) rotation; to help hitters get used to the feeling of rotating and pivoting their body without worrying about hitting the baseball.

Equipment: Bats

Coaching Key: Make sure that hitters' back leg and hip are rotating properly, with a strong pivot. Also be certain that hitters maintain their balance during the whole process and that their shoulders stay squared and level without any leaning or tilting.

How to Run It: Players get into a good hitting stance and then place the bat behind their back, horizontally through their elbows. The barrel of the bat should be on the players' dominant swing side. The players then line up facing you. As you wind up as though to pitch, the hitters go through their hitting process: get into the load position, pivot, and rotate their hips and torso while keeping the bat behind their back.

Extra Fun: Lead the drill with a windup motion but play "Simon Says" to see who the best listener is. For example, say, "Simon says turn your hips." The last player standing is the Batting Rotation Champion.

Drill 3. Basic Hitting-off-the-Tee Drill (ages 4-10)

Description: Players swing at a stationary ball (tee).

Goal: To develop a perfect, automatic swing, shifting body weight and generating bat speed.

Equipment: Tee, bats, and balls

Coaching Key: Players need to start in a balanced position, with hands, arms, and bat forming an upside down "V." Their shoulders should be level, and they should shift their weight to their back leg. They should then transfer their weight through their swing back. As they pivot, they should start moving the bat knob to the ball,

Balanced stance—shoulders level.

Hands and arms form upside down "V."

Transfer weight through swing back position—"Load."

Pivot and start the bat knob to ball. Eyes stay on ball.

Check swing plane position.

Head is still on target and bat comes through hitting zone level.

Follow through with head stationary and lower body balanced.

keeping their eyes on the ball. Their shoulders should stay straight and their hips rotate parallel to the target. Check their swing plane position and that the bat is level coming through the hitting zone. Check that through the extension and follow-through the head remains stationary and the lower body balanced.

How to Run It: This drill is run with one player at a time. Have the player go to the stationary tee and get ready to hit. Adjust the tee to different levels and depths to simulate different types of pitches and have the player swing at each position.

Extended Hitting-off-the-Tee Drill— Inside Pitch

Position the tee off the front leg of the hitter, simulating an inside pitch. Have the hitter bring the barrel of the bat close to his or her body, then make contact with the ball, and follow through. Contact with the baseball should be out in front of the lead foot. Keep in mind that the knob of the bat should go directly to the ball (knob to ball), which will let the player hit to the pull, or hitting, side of the field with authority. **(continued)**

Drills

Drill 3. Basic Hitting-off-the-Tee Drill (continued)

Extended Hitting-off-the-Tee Drill— Outside Pitch

Position the tee off the back leg of the hitter, simulating an outside pitch. To correctly hit an outside pitch the hitter must let the ball travel deep into the hitting zone before making contact with it, then extend the swing through the hitting zone. If done correctly the ball will be hit with force to the opposite field.

Extended Hitting-off-the-Tee Drill— High Pitch

Position the tee about chest high to the hitter, simulating a high pitch. To get on top of the baseball, and not hit a fly ball, the player needs to swing level or in a slightly downward plane. Have the hitter get the knob to the ball with the top hand down and extend through the hitting zone.

Extended Hitting-off-the-Tee Drill— Low Pitch

Position the tee about knee high to the hitter, simulating a low pitch. Have the hitter swing level and drive through the ball without dropping the shoulder and pulling out of his or her stance. Have the hitter continue extending the bat through the hitting zone after contact to prevent a weak ground ball or a pop-up.

Extended Hitting-off-the Tee Drill— Middle Pitch

Position the tee waist high to the hitter, simulating a pitch down the middle. Have the player put all of the hitting lessons into play to make a perfect swing at a perfect pitch.

Coaching Key Summary and Review:

 *Proper stance setup.*

 *Taking the load position.*

 *Putting knob to ball (downward plane).*

 *Balancing upper and lower body.*

 *Extending hands through contact.*

 *Following through with head and body balanced.*

Extra Fun: Players hit ground balls for distance. The player who hits the ball the farthest can pick his or her place in the batting lineup.

Drill 4. Soft Toss Drills (ages 6-10)

Regular Soft Toss

Description: Balls are softly tossed to batters to hit.

Goal: To make solid contact with the ball.

Equipment: Bat, bucket of 20 balls, net or screen

How to Run It: Stand four or five feet away from a hitter at a 45-degree angle. The coach should show

the batter the ball, then bring arm back and then forward to release the ball. The hitter should load back when the coach's arm comes back and start the swing when the ball is released ("when I go back, you go back"). Have the batter hit the ball on a downward plane, trying to hit line drives or hard ground balls.

Coaching Key: Develop good timing, making sure the hitter maintains balance throughout his swing. Instruct the hitter to get in the load position when your arm comes back and start his or her swing when you release the ball.

Advanced Variation: Toss five balls toward the hitter's back leg to simulate outside pitches. Then toss five balls toward the hitter's front leg to simulate inside pitches.

Open Hips Soft Toss

Description: The ball is softly tossed to players standing in an open-hip position.

Goal: To develop the proper swing by keeping hands inside the ball and extending through the hitting zone.

Equipment: Bat, bucket of 20 balls, net or screen

How to Run It: Have the hitter stand five to seven feet from the net (if needed) and at a 45-degree angle from you. The hitter's hips should be open to home plate. Sit on the bucket and toss the ball to the hitter, aiming at the spot where you would like the player to hit the ball. Before you toss the ball, show the batter the ball, then bring your arm back and release it.

Coaching Key: Work with the hitter on following the proper path to and through the hit and eliminating movement of the lower body. Have the hitter focus on using his or her hands to get the bat to the ball, keeping them inside the ball and extending as hard and fast as possible.

Extra Fun: On the 10th hit, the batter runs to first if the ball was hit to the infield and to second base if the ball was hit to the outfield.

Drills

Drill 5. Front Toss Drill (under- or overhand, ages 6-10)

Underhand toss.

Overhand toss.

Description: The ball is tossed softly toward the hitter, simulating real pitching.

Goal: To get batters accustomed to the feel of live pitching, with the ball coming directly toward them; to have batters use the big part of the field by tracking and then hitting a ball in different areas of the strike zone; to have batters shift body weight properly to achieve balance and timing; to have batters improve pitch-to-swing timing by going back in their swing as the pitcher's arm goes back to throw ("When I go back, you go back.").

Equipment: Bucket of balls, L -screen, players in the field to shag balls or batting cage

How to Run It:

As a line drive drill: Softly toss the ball at the player's belly button, simulating a pitch down the

middle of the plate. The hitter's objective should be to swing down on the baseball and hit a line drive back to the screen. This drill should be repeated at every practice so hitters consistently repeat the same fundamentally sound swing on a downward plane.

As an inside pitch drill: Toss the ball toward the hitter on the inner portion of the plate, simulating an

inside pitch. The hitter should aim to make contact with the baseball out in front of the plate. Remind hitters that they need to swing early and quickly rotate their hips with a strong "squash the bug" pivot. They must pull their hands inside the baseball and close to their body to make contact. After making contact they should extend their hands through the swing and follow through.

As an outside pitch drill: Toss the ball toward the outer portion of the plate, simulating an outside pitch. Hitters should work on making contact with the ball deep in the zone, so remind them to wait for the ball to come to them and see it in deep. Hitters should make contact with the ball from off the back hip, keeping the front of their body closed. To check for the right position before they start, have hitters touch their back knee to the ground.

Extra Fun: Batters who hit the net 10 times pick their position in the batting lineup.

Drill 6. Contact Point Drill (ages 6-10)

Description: Balls are softly tossed to batter to hit.

Goal: To consistently take a proper bat path to the ball.

Equipment: Bucket of 20 balls, stool, bat, and screen

How to Run It: Stand four or five feet from hitter at a 45-degree angle. Instruct the hitter to go to contact point and freeze. Then take same bat path back to the

STEP 2. Softly toss the ball.

load position. From the load position the instructor softly tosses the ball to hitter.

Coaching Key: Make sure the hitter is taking a downward path to the ball with the barrel staying above the hands. This enables the hitter to develop muscle memory and consistently make proper contact.

Extra Fun: On the 10th hit, the batter runs to first if the ball was hit to the infield and to second base if the ball was hit to the outfield.

STEP 1. Run through drill to contact point, then back to load position.

Drill 7. Hitting Stick Drill (ages 7-10)

Hitting stick at belt.

Head down, hips rotating.

Description: Players practice swinging the bat at belt level.

Goal: To develop a quick and repeatable swing that allows batters to maintain balance and generate power.

Equipment: Hitting stick and bat

How to Run It: Work with one player at a time. Hold out the hitting stick just in front of the hitter at his or her belt line. To hit the stick with the bat, the hitter should take the weight to the back of the body before exploding forward. Remind the hitter to keep his or her head down and eyes on the ball. The hitter's front foot and shoulder should go directly toward the target.

Coaching Key: Hitters should not drop their front shoulder or pull their head to the side.

Extra Fun: The first player who hits the stick 20 times in a row is the Contact Champion.

Front foot straight, follow through.

Drill 8. Hitting from Back to Front Drill (ages 7-10)

Description: Players practice tracking the ball from behind them to in front of them.

Goal: To have players keep their hands inside the baseball and wait until the last second to start their swing.

Equipment: Bucket of balls, stool, bat, and screen

How to Run It: Set up as though for a regular soft toss practice session but sit on a stool and toss the ball to the hitter from behind him or her, delivering it between the middle of the plate and the outside corner. Have the hitter concentrate on tracking the ball all the way to the bat through its straight-line path and wait for the ball to come to him or her before swinging.

Coaching Key: The majority of young hitters let their hands separate from their body when they swing, causing a loop-like swing instead of hitting all the way through. Hitters should keep the front of their body closed as long as possible and keep the barrel of the bat inside the ball. Otherwise they will hit the ball weakly or miss it entirely.

Extra Fun: The first hitter who hits 10 balls in a row is the Back-to-Front Champion.

Coach sits behind the hitter.

Hitter concentrates on the ball.

Coach throws to the middle of the plate, hitter keeps his eyes on the ball.

Stance stays balanced, hips open up.

Hitter pivots and hits through the ball.

Drills

Drill 9. Batting Practice (ages 7-10)

Description: Players practice hitting the ball to simulate playing in a game.

Goal: To accustom batters to hitting repeatedly, as in a game, at game speed; to help hitters develop eye-hand coordination by working with a pitcher or pitching machine, time pitches, and recognize different areas of the strike zone; to help players feel comfortable and safe in the batter's box and reduce their fear of being hit by a ball.

Equipment: L-screen, bucket of balls, players to field balls

How to Run It: Set up to throw 10 pitches to each player or have the player make five solid hits. Throw gentle overhand pitches from 30 feet away to players

Taking the load position.

Striding and "squashing the bug."

Making contact above the hands.

Extending.

Driving through the ball.

Touching the back with the bat.

six and under. For children six to nine, pitches should be thrown under 40 miles an hour from 40 feet away by either you, a player, or a pitching machine. Use age-appropriate baseballs (if you're unsure what's appropriate, start with Little League tee balls and move up when ready) and make sure to supervise if a player is pitching.

Coaching Key: During this drill, limit your

coaching and instructing. When you hold this practice, players should already have gotten plenty of instruction, so let them practice what you taught them.

Extra Fun: Batting practice is usually when players have the most fun, but you can also hold a Home Run Derby, in which line drives over second base count as home runs.

Drill 10. Guess the Pitch Drill (ages 7-10)

Description: Players try to guess whether a strike or a ball is being pitched.

Goal: To help players visualize balls and strikes and the correct hitting process.

Equipment: Bats

How to Run It: Have the players form a circle around you and assume the proper hitting stance. Go into a windup and pretend to throw a pitch while say-

ing "strike" or "ball." Tell the batters to swing only when you say "strike."

Coaching Key: Have the batters work on the proper stance and swing without worrying about hitting the ball.

Extra Fun: The last player to swing at a strike or anyone who swings at a ball is out of the drill. The last player remaining is the winner.

Drill 11. Shave the Fence Drill (ages 7-10)

Description: Batters practice hitting standing next to the fence.

Goal: To consistently take a proper, mechanically sound swing. If the hitter's swing breaks down, the hitter will have instant feedback, because he or she will hit the fence with the bat.

Equipment: Bat

How to Run it: Have the hitter align with the fence close to it. Have the hitter hold the knob in the belt area with the bat facing straight out toward the fence. Then have the hitter go through the hitting process at real speed. To swing properly, hitters must keep their hands inside the ball. They must lead with the knob, with the front of the body staying closed. The bat should pass the fence without making contact with it. The follow-through should be done while maintaining balance.

Coaching Key: If the hitter consistently hits the fence it is because his or her swing has a loop in it. Remind players to keep their hands inside and to extend the bat barrel out in front of them. Make sure the front of hitters' bodies stays closed and that they "squash the bug" to rotate properly. This drill is beneficial for hitters who extend their hands and arms too quickly.

Extra Fun: The batter who takes the most swings without hitting the fence gets to choose where he or she would like to bat in the next game.

Set up. *Load/weight shift.* *Swing.* *Follow through.*

Drill 12. Pepper Drill (ages 7-10)

Description: Players hit a Whiffle ball back to the fielder who threw it.

Goal: To help players develop bat control and accuracy.

Equipment: Bat, Whiffle ball, and gloves

How to Run It: Line up three to five fielders side by side, facing one batter who is 12 to 15 feet away. Have one fielder throw the Whiffle ball to the batter, throwing it nice and easy so the batter can hit it. The batter should try to hit a soft ground ball back to the fielder who threw it. Each pitcher should take a turn throwing to the batter.

Coaching Key: Have batters concentrate on swinging softly and hitting the ball right toward the pitcher.

Extra Fun: The batter becomes a pitcher after he or she misses hitting the ball three times or the ball is caught. Fielder #1 becomes the new batter.

Drill 13. Grounders Drill (ages 7-10)

Description: Players practice hitting ground balls.

Goal: To have hitters stay on top of the ball.

Equipment: Bat, bucket of balls, gloves, and helmet

How to Run It: Have one batter in the batter's box and five players in the infield. Pitch to the batter as long as he or she keeps hitting ground balls or line drives. After five hits, have the batter run it out until thrown out or making it to home plate.

Coaching Key: Be certain batters get into the proper hitting stance and are wearing a helmet.

Extra Fun: The player who get the most hits without being thrown out is King of the Mound.

Drill 14. One-Arm-Swing Drill (ages 7-10)

Description: Players practice swinging the bat properly but use only one hand.

Goal: To build players' hand strength for better bat control.

Equipment: Light bat and bucket of balls

How to Run It: Have the hitters choke up or use a small bat before getting in the correct batting stance. When the ball is pitched to them have them swing, holding the bat with their bottom hand only. Then have them switch and swing with the top hand only.

Coaching Key: Make sure that players use the right swing mechanics.

Extra Fun: Have five batters swing 15 times each using only one hand. The one who makes the most hits wins. If there's a tie, the one who hit the ball the farthest wins.

Drills

Drill 15. Hit the Spot Drill (ages 7-10)

Description: Players try to hit the dot on the baseball.

Goal: To help players keep their eyes on the ball.

Equipment: Bat, bucket of balls, and gloves

How to Run It: Have five fielders and one hitter for this drill. Draw a quarter-size red or blue dot on some but not all of the baseballs. Then

throw balls or use a tee for players to hit the balls. Have them tell you which pitches were "dot balls."

Coaching Key: Remind players to keep their eyes on the ball all the way to the bat.

Extra Fun: The player who correctly distinguishes the most dot balls from the other balls out of 10 pitches wins the Eagle Eye Award.

Drill 16. Game Winner Drill (ages 7-10)

Description: Players simulate game play.

Goal: To have players learn to play in game conditions.

Equipment: Bat, bucket of balls, and gloves

How to Run It: Put one player at each defensive position except catcher and pitcher. Stand on the pitching mound and pitch to the hitters. Each hitter who misses or takes a called third strike is out. Players who hit foul balls continue to hit. When a ball is put in play, have the batter

run to first base. Have the fielders try to make outs.

Coaching Key: Be sure to rotate players for this drill. Have batters go to left field and rotate clockwise until they reach third base. At that point it's their turn to bat again.

Extra Fun: After every batter has hit, those who reached first can hit again. All the others stay in the field. Continue the drill until the last hitter becomes the Game Winner Champion.

Drill 17. Rapid Fire Drill (ages 7-10)

Description: Balls are quickly thrown to players to develop concentration and a quick swing.

Goal: To reinforce the need to bring the hands quickly to the ball.

Equipment: Bat, bucket of balls, and gloves

How to Run It: For this drill, one player hits and five are in the field. Have the hitter get into the proper stance and kneel four or five feet away from him or her at a 45-degree angle. Softly and quickly toss balls

to the hitter so that they begin at the top of the strike zone and drop toward the front of the plate.

Coaching Key: Toss the balls quickly to force batters to concentrate and swing fast. Remind batters to hit on a downward arc.

Extra Fun: Have the batter keep hitting until he or she misses three in a row. After 10 hits in a row, have the batter rotate to the field.

Drill 18. Mini Whiffle Ball Drill (ages 7-10)

Description: Players try to hit balls that are smaller than baseballs.

Goal: To develop and improve young hitters' eye-hand coordination by using small balls that are harder to make contact with and that can change direction easily because of the small holes that let air through.

Equipment: Bat (a hitting stick is optional) and 10 to 15 Whiffle "golf balls" (1")

How to Run It: Pitch to players using small Whiffle balls. Have hitters keep their eyes on the ball

through contact and be ready to adjust if the ball changes direction. To increase the difficulty of the drill, have players use a hitting stick or thin bat.

Coaching Key: Make sure hitters track the ball all the way to the bat. Also remind them to shift their weight and stay balanced because Whiffle balls can change direction at any time during a toss.

Extra Fun: Have one player hit and two others try to catch the Whiffle balls at a safe distance. Rotate players after 10 hits.

In the ready position, eyes on the ball.

Loading back, shifting weight.

Shifting weight forward, swinging on level plane through the ball.

APPENDIX

Appendix A

A Note About Baseball from One Generation to the Next

It was a hot and dusty afternoon, but there we were in brand-new gray uniforms with bright yellow trim. We stood on an all-dirt field, lined with chalk, with official bases, a backstop, an outfield fence, and bleachers. There were spectators and our families—and they were cheering for us, their teams!

Little League had come to my hometown. For the first time ever, kids were playing "real" baseball. It was great! The day after our first game, the Times Herald featured the Grand Opening dedication and a picture of me taking a really big swing—and missing! But I was in print, playing baseball.

My buddies and I loved sports. They had made a huge difference in our lives, and finally we had the chance to look and play like the big guys. We moved from pick-up and sandlot games to being very special players. We even began to think like a team: Where do I need to be to make that play? How can I back up Bruce and Carlos in the infield? How do those other guys feel when they lose? Suddenly the game was not all about me—I was part of something much bigger than my 11-year-old self. I was part of a team.

My first year in Little League was a big learning experience. I thought I was a really good player, but Little League put that picture in focus. During one game I was daydreaming in right field. Then I saw the batter swing and heard the crack of the bat. It was my chance! I ran in to catch that powerful line-drive fly—and the ball sailed five feet over my outstretched glove. As I came off the field, people shouted, "What's the matter? Can't you see the ball?!"

So I got glasses. And I started paying much better attention. I also started listening better—to my coaches, my friends, and my parents. And I learned about hard work. I began to understand that if I practiced, I really did get better. I hit better. I was a better baseman. I was quicker in the field. I even felt better about myself.

In the second year I played first base and batted third in the lineup. I had started to think baseball. I thought like a team player, and so did my friends. Mickey was our catcher. When there was an infield hit, Mickey would run like the devil to back me up at first base. Most of the time he got there before the runner. I was grateful and very inspired. I wanted to run that fast.

At the end of that season an award ceremony was held. My mom and dad came—a big deal for me—and my teammates and I were excited and nervous. We had never been to a baseball award ceremony before, and we didn't know what to expect. We did know, though, that "Jojo" White, a real, live, professional baseball player and coach, would be there to give out the awards.

I still have the award I won. It is a small round sphere about the size of an orange, with red stitching along the seams. It's no longer new, but a bit scuffed—a baseball hit a few times, and caught and thrown a few times, to first base. When I turn that baseball over in my hands, I can still read the names of the men who signed it: Dusty Rhodes, Alvin Dark, Hank Thompson, Sal Maglie—the greats of the 1954 World Champion New York Giants baseball team. I was given that award for being the Most Improved Player on our team and being selected to the All Star Team. When Jojo White handed it to me, he said, "Play hard, with all your heart. Be the best that you can be."

I plan to give this little round sphere of achievement and happiness to my son Ken, who loves the game of baseball the way I do. I will give it to him because he is a good man and because he not only has a passion for the game but a passion to mentor and help young players develop skills and love the game too. I will also give it to him because he has a son—a son who has a brand-new uniform and who loves to play baseball on the Little League team his dad coaches. Today I assist his dad and the other coaches and greatly enjoy being part of another wonderful learning and mentoring experience related to baseball. Someday, perhaps, my son will be an assistant coach for his son, and the love of baseball—and the special baseball I was awarded—will be passed on to and treasured by him and generations to come.

Jim Siegler

Appendix B: Standard Equipment List

Equipment List

1. Metal net with pull rope to drag field
2. Rake (metal or plastic)
3. Broom and small brush
4. Multiple bags of ready-made infield dirt
5. Chalk, liner machine, and string
6. Hose and water outlet
7. Pitching machine with accessible power
8. Removable bases
9. Extra set of catcher equipment
10. First aid kit
11. Hammer, pliers, and screwdrivers
12. Tee
13. Knee pads
14. Hang-up bag for helmets
15. Six helmets
16. Six bats
17. Two sets of catcher's equipment
18. Catcher's mitt
19. Two extra fielding mitts
20. 36 to 48 practice baseballs
21. Baseball bucket

Appendix C: Facilities Checklist

Facilities Checklist

Field Surface
☐ Field grass is level or cut.
☐ The field is free from toxic substances (lime, Fertilizer, etc.).
☐ The field is free of low spots.
☐ The playing surface is free of debris.
☐ No large rocks are on the field.
☐ The field is free of protruding objects other than bases.
☐ Any minor potential hazard in the field of play is marked with a cone or chalk.
☐ The field is not too wet or has standing water.
☐ The field lines are well marked for game play.
☐ Outfield fences have a warning track marked with chalk.

Outside Playing Area
☐ The edge of the playing field is safely away from trees, walls, fences,and cars.
☐ Storage sheds and facilities are locked after play.
☐ The dugout area (ground surface and equipment) is in safe condition.
☐ The fences or walls lining the area are in good repair.

Spectator Areas
☐ Areas for spectators are clearly marked and spectators are advised to be alert at all times.

Equipment
☐ The backstop is secured to the ground.
☐ The backstop is well behind the playing area.

Appendix D: Sample Consent Form

Informed Consent Form

I hereby give my permission for _____ to participate in _____ during the athletic season beginning on _____. Further, I authorize the school, league, or club to provide emergency treatment of any injury or illness my child may experience if qualified medical personnel consider treatment necessary and perform the treatment. This authorization is granted only if I cannot be reached and a reasonable effort has been made to do so.

Parent or Guardian: _____

Address: _____ **Phone:** ( ) _____

Cell phone: ( ) _____ **Other number:** ( ) _____

Additional contact in case of emergency: _____

Relationship: _____ **Phone:** ( ) _____

Family physician: _____ **Phone:** ( ) _____

Medical conditions (e.g., allergies, chronic illness): _____

_____

_____

_____

My child and I are aware that participating in _____ is a potentially hazardous activity. We assume all risks associated with participation in this sport, including but not limited to falls, contact with other participants, the effects of the weather or traffic, and other reasonable-risk conditions associated with the sport. All such risks to my child are known and appreciated by my child and me.

We understand this informed consent form and agree to its conditions.

Childs signature: _____ **Date:** _____

Parent's or guardian's signature: _____ **Date:** _____

Appendix E: Sample Emergency Information Card

Emergency Information Card

Player's name: _____ Date of birth: _____

Address: _____

_____ Phone: (   ) _____

Contact Information

Parent's or guardian's name: _____

Address: _____

_____

Phone: (   ) _____ Other phone: (   ) _____

Additional contact's name: _____

Relationship to player: _____

Address: _____

_____

Phone: (   ) _____ Other phone: (   ) _____

Insurance Information:

Name of insurance company: _____

Policy name and number: _____

Medical Information:

Physician's name: _____ Phone: (   ) _____

Is your child allergic to any drugs? Yes☐ No☐. If so, what? _____

Does your child have other allergies? _____

_____

Does your child have any of the following? Asthma Diabetes Epilepsy

Is your child taking medications? Yes☐ No☐. If so, what? _____

_____

Does your child wear contact lenses? Yes☐ No☐.

Is there additional information we should know about your child's health or

physical condition? Yes☐ No☐. If yes, please explain: _____

_____

Parent's or guardian's signature: _____ Date: _____

© The Official Handbook of USA Baseball

Appendix F: Sample Conflict Resolution Letter

Dear parents,

It is the wish of the Little League board that everyone connected with the league has a fun and positive season. Little League will probably be one of the most enjoyable experiences of your child's life, and perhaps of your life as well. There is nothing that quite matches the excitement of a Little League game!

Occasionally, however, a conflict can arise among participants in Little League. For example, a parent may not approve of the actions of a manager or coach, or a manager or coach may not handle a certain player's attitude or actions. Or, perhaps, an umpire may not cope with a particular parent's response to a ruling. As infrequently as these situations occur, they can be quite distressing to all involved, particularly the children, and can take the fun out of the game.

Our board wants very much for such conflicts to be resolved quickly, objectively, and equitably, with the highest consideration given to the welfare of the children.

Therefore, the board has provided the following conflict resolution process. It was designed for and should be followed by all league participants, including managers, coaches, players, umpires, parents, and spectators.

1. If you do not approve of the actions or attitude of another, bring it to the person's attention quickly, in a courteous and positive manner. Avoid discussing your disapproval of an adult volunteer in front of any child—doing so will prevent undermining the authority of the adult, which is an essential part of the Little League program. Always approach the adult volunteer discreetly and privately, raising your concern person to person. When approached promptly and with sensitivity to the feelings of others, many problems quickly become non-issues and a higher degree of cooperation and understanding is achieved between the parties.

2. If you cannot achieve what seems to be the right outcome, consult with your division player agent, who will listen objectively and impartially and take action that he or she feels is appropriate. Division player agents are members of the Little League board and will respect your privacy in the matter.

3. If your issue is still not resolved, raise it with the Little League board of directors. Only matters of the greatest concern should be brought to the board, and only after the means above have been exercised in good faith. The board will respect your privacy and, at its discretion, appoint a committee of board members who can remain objective to arbitrate the matter. If a division player agent or board member is involved in the conflict, he or she will not be included as an arbiter in the conflict resolution process. When a matter is brought before the board, all decisions of the board or its appointed committee are binding and the matter is considered resolved.

Any action connected with Little League that you deem illegal, immoral, or unethical should be reported to a board member at once.

The league thanks you in advance for your cooperation.

Sincerely,

© Little League Baseball

Appendix G: Sample Standards of Conduct

Standards of Conduct

Standards of conduct exist for all participants in this league. It is in everyone's interest that you read, understand, and comply with them. Please raise any questions you have with these standards with the board of directors of the league.

Rights of Players
- To participate in playing baseball regardless of skill level, but at a skill level that is commensurate with the player's ability level
- To play baseball as a child and not as an adult, and to have fun
- To have qualified adult leaders who clearly communicate what is expected of each player
- To receive proper preparation for playing the game and to learn the skills of the game
- To learn to be a member of the team
- To be treated with dignity by all personal involved in the game
- To participate in a safe and healthy environment

Responsibilities of Players
- To attend all practices and games on time and to have the proper equipment
- To try their very best at all times, win or lose
- To obey adult authorities (managers, coaches, umpires) and to be respectful at all times
- To learn to be a team player, choosing the team's goals over personal goals
- To be a good sport and to abide by the rules of the game at all times
- To respect their teammates' rights as well as the rights of players on opposing teams

Rights of Parents
- To participate in assisting the team in a meaningful way
- To have an open path of communication with managers, coaches, and board members and to know and support what is expected of their child
- To have a responsive and effective process for expressing concerns about the league program, team leadership, or any other matter
- To understand the rules of the game for each division and for the league
- To expect support from the league board consistent with the policies and procedures of the league and with local rules

Responsibilities of Parents
- To learn the rules of the game for each division and for the league
- o participate in some constructive way in the league
- To support the managers, coaches, and other adult volunteers by ensuring their children are obedient and cooperative at all times
- To treat all volunteers (managers, coaches, umpires, board members, etc.) and all players with dignity
- To be a model of good sportsmanship
- To urge their children and other children to put their best effort into everything they do
- To refrain from the use of alcohol, tobacco, abusive language, and inappropriate conduct while attending any Little League function

© Little League Baseball

Notes

Notes

796.357077 SIE
Siegler, Kenneth.
Teaching hitting
 fundamentals

WARREN TWP LIBRARY
   42 MOUNTAIN BLVD

      SEP 1 0 2008

   WARREN, NJ 070
      908-754-5554

YOUTH BASEBALL BOOK

Teaching Hitting Fundamentals

Parent and coaching guide will get your young ball player off to the right start.

- *Instead of spending $150.00 dollars on a bat spend $24.95 on how to use it!*

- *Help your child be a hitter while developing lifelong character.*

- *Jam-packed color action photos that show right way to coach and develop a swing.*

Order yours today at: amazon.com/books and search Kenneth Siegler Youth Baseball. Call 650.216.6089 with any questions.

Coaching Youth Baseball
Teaching Hitting Fundamentals
Developing Hitters with Character
By Kenneth Siegler